\ FOUR WHO SPOKE OUT /
Burke, Fox, Sheridan, Pitt

by
Robert T. Oliver

Biography Index Reprint Series

BOOKS FOR LIBRARIES PRESS
FREEPORT, NEW YORK

CONTENTS

Part One
Their Place in History

Part Two
Their Audience

Part Three
Their Character

Part Four
Their Methods

Part Five
Retrospect

Appendix A Biographical Table
Appendix B Bibliographical Note

For

E. S. O. and K. A. O.

*We wander in our thousands over the
face of the earth, the illustrious and
the obscure, earning beyond the seas
our fame, our money, or only a crust
of bread; but it seems to me that for
each of us going home must be like
going to render an account. We return to face our superiors, our kin-
dred, our friends—those whom we
obey, and those whom we love.*

—From Joseph Conrad

FOREWORD

The eighteenth century was the seedbed of much that is characteristic of our age: belief in progress, respect for the dignity and rights of the common man, rationalism in religion, the triumph of science and reason over traditionalism, the slow growth of internationalism. In many respects, the four decades covered in this book offer sources or parallels to much that has happened in our own time. A concise study of that formative period is of interest to many readers today — especially since we are looking earnestly for solid foundations upon which to build a new order.

The twentieth century is witnessing the tremendous influence exercised by men of powerful speech — by Lenin in directing the Russian Revolution, by Mussolini and Hitler in stirring up the storm of Fascist reaction, and by Churchill and Roosevelt in arousing the force of liberalism to counteract it. The latter years of the eighteenth century were also a period in which powerful currents of reaction and reform were shaped, directed, and illuminated in the eloquent speeches of parliamentary orators. In this book, an effort is made to assess the means by which the four greatest speakers of that time exercised their influence over the English Parliament and nation — and thereby upon the world. Historians, political scientists, and students of speech will be interested in the study of the personalities and techniques of the four great speakers who are discussed in these pages.

Into this book have gone indirectly the labors of many men, some of whom are listed in the bibliography. The author has drawn especially heavily upon the many keen observers of the late eighteenth century who registered their observations in diaries, letters, and books. With the benefit of their contemporary view, he has sought to avoid the danger of chronological astigmatism. Rather than looking back upon the period, he has tried to picture it as it appeared to its own contemporaries. This is especially important in considering the relations of the speakers to their audiences. To the extent that the attempt has succeeded, the credit is due to the many diarists and historians who have been consulted.

More personally, the author would like to acknowledge his great debt of gratitude to the scholars who have guided and encouraged his interest in the period. To Dr. Robert Horn, of the University of Oregon, and to Professor Harry Hayden Clark, and Dr. Henry Lee Ewbank, of the University of Wisconsin, special thanks are due. The author is also conscious of many benefits accruing to the manuscript from the keen and spirited criticisms of his wife.
Syracuse, New York
February, 1946

Part One

Their Place in History

Chapter 1 – Rich Traditions

When London Cockneys, with German bombers roaring overhead in 1940 and robot bombs falling in 1945, sang, "There'll always be an England," they were not only prophecying the future, but were also drawing upon the rich traditions of a valiant past. England had fought for her life before, and she had been heartened on previous occasions by the great utterances of courageous leaders, just as Winston Churchill's inspired eloquence helped maintain the spirit to hold on and pull through in the dismal months of 1940 and 1941.

There is much in England's past that Englishmen, and Americans, too, may consider with advantage in facing the problems of today and tomorrow. Particularly do the last forty years of the eighteenth century provide many fruitful parallels with the first half of the twentieth. Then, as now, were there depressions and wars. That period, like the present, was an era of struggle between liberalism and

1

reaction.   As in our own day, that was a time of "one
worldliness," when the problems of Europe, America, and
the Orient were inextricably intertwined.   Then, as now,
the contending forces were led by men whose motives,
abilities, and methods were all-important in determining the
course of events. As we have had Hitler, they had
Napoleon. The ideal we are seeking – of nations united in
war and in peace – was likewise a need for them. The fear
of a Europe united not with, but against, the Anglican race
was a bogey then, as now.

From the period of the American Revolution and the
Napoleonic wars, we have much to learn. From the dynamic
spokesmen of that time we readily draw conclusions of value
in guiding our thinking today. A detailed analysis of the
character and methods of the men whose influence contributed greatly in shaping modern England has a purpose
to serve for us.   In the statesmen of that day, we find
patterns we may usefully study in assessing our own leaders.
In their problems, we see mirrored many of our own issues,
with the outlines of the former all the clearer because of
the fading of contemporary prejudices and emotions. From
their speeches, we hear many echoes bearing directly upon
our own times.

*"To tax and to please, any more than to love and to be
wise, is not given to men.*

*"In this country no man, in consequence of his riches or
rank, is so high as to be above the reach of the laws, and
no individual is so poor or inconsiderable as not to be within
their protection.*

*"Magnanimity in politics is not seldom the truest wis-
dom; and a great empire and little minds go ill together.*

"Men will not suffer bad things because their ancestors have suffered worse.

"It is a peace of which everybody is glad and no one is proud.

"Let us continue to hope till events compel us to despair.

"England has saved herself by her exertions; let us hope that she will save Europe by her example.

"No single man can save the country. If a nation depends only upon one man, it cannot, and, I will add, it does not deserve to be saved; it can only be done by the Parliament and the people."

The history of that period is the seedbed from which many of our modern institutions and beliefs have been harvested. It was then that the old feudal society was finally challenged and eventually broken up. Modern industrialism was being born. Democracy developed from a theoretical dream described in philosophical treatises to the living reality of legislative halls and battle fields. The rights of free speech, a free press, and freedom of religion were at last effectively asserted. The last struggle in England was waged between absolute monarchy and a responsible Parliament. The foundations of the new Commonwealth were laid. The four decades from 1765 to 1806 were gloomy, reactionary, and distraught—but at their close the new liberalism had gained a force it was never thereafter to lose.

During that period, the English Empire crumbled and all but dissolved. The thirteen American colonies endured accumulated abuses that finally caused them to rebel. Ireland came near to an independence that finally slipped from her grasp and was not recovered until the Treaty of Versailles. The new English dependencies in India were cynically exploited and robbed, until at last the English conscience was aroused. And, for the first time in England, that conscience found a support on which it could grow — an articulate public opinion. First by mobs storming through London's streets — then in newspapers and public meetings — the people found a means of making themselves heard. In such a time, uncertainly, gropingly, with many retrogressions, democracy was born.

.Not least in importance among the forces operating during those four decades were four orators in whose words the history of the age was partly created and is brilliantly illumined. They were the prime spokesmen of the new order. Their influence helped it to arise. They fought on the floor of Parliament for the American Revolutionists, for extension of the ballot, for abolition of the trade in slaves. They cried out for the right of all men to speak and write whatever opinions they might hold, for justice to Ireland, India, and English Catholics, for the basic rights of individualism and the dignity of man which created democracy as we know it today. What Napoleon was on the battlefield, Burke, Fox, Sheridan and Pitt were on the floor of Parliament. Lovers of either democracy or of eloquence will find much of significance in their personalities, their speeches, and the causes in which they fought.

Edmund Burke entered Parliament in 1765, a mature scholar of books and of life, at the age of thirty-five. Charles James Fox, accomplished Oxonian student, Parisian dandy, and London gambler, cheated the election laws to slip in three years later at the age of nineteen. A decade and more passed while these two fought their oratorical battles, first as enemies, then as friends, until the election of 1780 brought in their two compeers. Richard Brinsley

Sheridan came into Parliament with a ripe fame as a successful dramatist, but with his ability as a statesman and speaker still to be developed. William Pitt, at twenty-one, was already master of that eloquence which in four years made him prime minister of England, and enabled him to hold that position for substantially the rest of his life.

Burke resigned from Parliament in 1794; Pitt and Fox both died in 1806; and Sheridan by that year had lost his political and oratorical prestige. The four decades which encompassed their fame were glorious in word, if often infamous in deed. Without these four men the deeds would have been much more infamous – the words less glorious by far.

Chapter 2 – Their England

The England that went through the ferment of the seventeenth century emerged into the eighteenth anxious for quiet, comfort, and peace. The wars of the Commonwealth and the quarrels with the later Stuarts were ended in 1688 when William and Mary were called from Holland to assume the throne. Under them and their successor, Queen Anne, England forgot the dissentions which had divided her people into Puritan and Loyalist camps. For the upper classes the jolly days described by the *Spectator Papers* were ushered in. The English Squirearchy was pleased to turn its attention from political warfare to fox hunting and the new sociability of the coffee houses. War they now considered as an occasional and distant adventure, to be fought across the Channel, where it did not constantly endanger the safety and security of their own homes. Politics lost its partisan bitterness through a coup of the Whigs, who jealously guarded the deathbed of the dying Queen Anne, and called over the petty ruler of Hanover to become, as George I, their puppet King. The Tories were routed and Robert

Walpole commenced his long one-party rule, in which all political disputes were healingly salved with liberal applications of bribery.

By 1742, however, the political truce was ended and Walpole was driven from office. Once more the government became a prize sought by contending politicians. Walpole's chief foe had been the upstart William Pitt – later to become Earl of Chatham – a brilliant speaker, but without influential family connections or much partisan support. The prize of political power, however, went for a time to another Whig politician who was no less corrupt than Walpole, and far less able, the Duke of Newcastle. Remaining behind scenes, in the best tradition of political bossism, Newcastle presented the office of prime minister to his brother, Henry Pelham, who held it eleven years, until his death in 1754.

Meanwhile, England had been engaged in recurrent warfare, fighting to gain ascendancy over France, and to extend her colonial empire. In both aims she was successful, but at a frightful cost in money and lives. Of the one hundred twenty-seven years which elapsed between the Revolution of 1688 and the battle of Waterloo, England spent sixty-four of them, or more than half of the whole time, at war.[1]

---

1. England took part in the following seven wars:
   1. "King William's War," 1689-1697.
   2. The War of the Spanish Succession, 1702-1713.
   3. The War of the Austrian Succession, 1739-1748.
   4. The Seven Years War, 1756-1763.
   5. The War of the American Revolution, 1775-1783.
   6, 7. Two wars with France, 1793-1802; and 1803-1815.

The national debt was piling up at a fearful rate, and continued to increase throughout the century.[2]

The situation demanded a strong and capable control which Newcastle was unable to provide. He quarrelled with his political partner, Henry Fox (the father of Charles James Fox) and was forced to relinquish control of the government in 1756. Then the Elder Pitt, in his forty-eighth year, without partisan support, was literally forced upon the king by the strength of public opinion. It proved to be an amazingly good solution for the governmental problems of England. The Seven Years War had commenced just before Newcastle left office. Pitt was not a soldier, but he proved to be an excellent civilian commander. His policy was to select his generals for their ability, rather than for their social standing, and to provide abundant men and supplies for their needs. The war was carried on in America, in Africa, in India, and in Europe, and England was successful on all four continents. In the midst of victories of unparalleled brilliance, George II died, and George III came to the throne, determined to oust his powerful and

*2. A few figures will illustrate the problems arising from the increase of debt:

In 1756 the national debt was £				74,575,025
In 1763 "	"	"	"	132,716,049
In 1775 "	"	"	"	126,843,811
In 1783 "	"	"	"	231,843,641
In 1793 "	"	"	"	247,674,434
In 1802 "	"	"	"	537,673,008

These figures are taken from "Public Income and Expenditures, 1688-1869" published by the House of Commons, July 29, 1869. They should be read in the light of the declining value of the £, which did not, however, substantially change their general import.

popular minister, and to gather the ruling powers in his own hands. His interference in the war soon accomplished this end, and Pitt resigned in October, 1760.

The instability of the succeeding governments may be illustrated by a simple enumeration of them. Of the fourteen ministries which succeeded before the death of the second Pitt and of Fox in 1806, only two (the ministries of North and the Younger Pitt) possessed any real stability and power. The remainder were merely attempts at adjustment:

> Newcastle, (Whig), 1761 to May, 1762.
> Bute (Tory), May 1762 to April, 1763.
> Grenville (Whig), April, 1763 to July, 1765.
> Rockingham (Whig), July, 1765 to August, 1766.
> The Elder Pitt (Whig), August, 1766 to December, 1768.
> Grafton (Whig), December, 1768 to January, 1770.
> North (Tory), January, 1770 to March, 1782.
> Rockingham (Whig), March-July, 1782.
> Shelburne (Whig), July, 1782 to February, 1783.
> Portland (The Fox-North Coalition), April-December, 1783.
> The Younger Pitt (Tory), December, 1783 to February, 1801.
> Addington (Tory), February, 1801 to May, 1803.
> The Younger Pitt (Tory), May, 1803 to January 23, 1806.
> Ministry of All the Talents (largely Whig), January, 1806 to September 13, 1806

Although definite party denominations are given to the ministeries, these are descriptive rather than prescriptive. The "Old Whigs," based upon the principle of rule by the aristocratic families, were breaking up. The Elder Pitt was an independent Whig and the Grenville and Grafton ministeries were also of this character. Rockingham's sector of the Whigs belonged to the "old" school, but had an infusion of new liberalism. Shelburne was in the Pitt tradition of the Whig party, but was more cordial in his relation to

the King. Bute and North were Tories in the strict sense
that they believed in the principle of rule by the King. The
Younger Pitt went into office with liberal pretensions, but
was forced to conform to his Tory majority.

Despite the strict limitation of the suffrage, Parliament's
avowed independence of the public will, and the subversive
measures adopted by the reactionaries at the close of the
century, a reform movement did arise, and actually exercised considerable effect upon legislation. In Ireland, for instance, legislative independence was won in 1782 and was
exercised until 1800, in which year Pitt managed through
systematic corruption to win enough votes to pass the Act
of Union. Ireland had to wait until after World War I
to regain a similar amount of freedom. Strong and repeated
movements were instigated to repeal the test and corporation
acts, aimed at the protestant dissenters, and to gain political
emancipation for the Catholics. Some concessions were won,
such as the freedom of Catholic priests from arrest for
preaching, and the right of Catholics to serve in the army.
Complete religious freedom, however, was postponed for
several decades by the phobia accompanying the French
wars. The growing strength of the movement to abolish
the slave trade, which finally triumphed in 1807, came
chiefly from outside the House of Commons. It was only
due to insistent and wide-spread demands from the public
that Burke was enabled to pass his bill in 1782 diminishing
the number of sinecures, and greatly limiting other forms
of corruption and waste.

Electoral reform became a prime issue, due principally to
the influence of public opinion. The Duke of Richmond,
leader of the Whigs in the House of Lords, talked of

universal suffrage, equal electoral districts, and annual Parliaments. The Whigs, cut off from any support from the throne, were forced to adopt electoral reform as one of their planks. The Foxites took up the cry for annual Parliaments, which might be elected even oftener if need be, and so came to be called Oftener-if-need-bes. Wilkes anticipated the Reform Bill of the next century by proposing to disfranchise the "rotten" boroughs, and to distribute their representation among the counties and populous towns. Strangely enough, part of the opposition to this movement came from the large towns themselves, which dreaded the rioting and disturbance to trade that inevitably accompanied elections. When the younger Pitt entered Parliament in 1781, he pledged himself to the cause of electoral reform, and only abandoned it after several failures convinced him that he was jeopardizing his position as prime minister and leader of the Tory party. Sheridan fought valiantly for several years for a reform of the representation of the Scotch boroughs, though his underlying motive must have been even more to undermine the powerful influence of the Scotch politician, Henry Dundas, than to aid the people. Such was Dundas's character, however, that the two motives were in complete harmony. The electoral reform movement was taken up by Charles Grey when he entered Parliament, and was urged by him in the 90's, until the reaction against Jacobinism made such a proposal absolutely hopeless. He later renewed his efforts, however, and finally won passage of the Reform Bill of 1832.

Reform of taxation was also accomplished during this period, including adoption of an income tax, and taxation of sinecures, pensions, and places. Furthermore, the old practice of granting douceurs and heavy rates of interest to friends of the minister for governmental loans was largely discontinued under the second Pitt, and thereafter open bids were received from potential lenders. Such financial reforms as these were won largely because of public outcries against the war-time taxation burden.

Public opinion, of course, was neither omniscient, nor all-powerful. The American war was at first favored by the English public, and a reversion of feeling was brought about partly through the power of Whig oratory in the House of Commons. Likewise, reform of the government of India and of the whole colonial policy, although it vitally affected the welfare of England, was too remote a problem to arouse public feeling. Burke and his friends had first to convince the public of the need of reform, in order that thereafter this public feeling might be used as a weapon to force Parliament to act. Measures of economic reform, which surpassed the understanding of the public, and of most members of Parliament as well, were effected through the influence of Adam Smith and the determination of Pitt.

Of other reforms there were not many. Almost unbelievable, (until we remember that times and morals change) was the neglect by public interest of a large number of prevalent abuses which closely affected the people. A mere glance at a few of them will illustrate that humanitarianism and feelings of social responsibility were still weak.

The navy. The French wars demanded a constantly increasing number of seamen who, on account of bad food, bad treatment, and poor pay after they entered the service, were hard to secure. Pitt was forced to have recourse to "pressing" or kidnapping men from the streets, taverns docks, ships, – even from the ships of foreign countries (a practice that led directly to the War of 1812) – to supply the demands of the navy. Herman Melville, in his book *Israel Potter*, described the conditions with heightened rhetoric, but without exaggeration of the facts:

"Still more, *that* was a period when the uttermost resources of England were taxed to the quick; when the masts of her multiplied fleets almost transplanted her forests, all standing to the sea; when British press gangs not only boarded foreign pierheads, but boarded their own merchantmen at the mouth of the Thames, and boarded the very firesides along its banks; when Englishmen were knocked down and dragged into the Navy, like cattle into the slaughter-house, with every mortal provocation to a mad desperation against the service that thus ran their unwilling heads into the muzzles of the enemy's cannon."

Yet, the reform of this situation came neither from the Parliament, nor the public, but from the sailors themselves, in the form of the worst crime on shipboard: mutiny. In the dark days of 1797, when accumulated misfortunes threatened to end England's power as a great nation, the sailors mutinied at the Nore and at Spithead, and the government was forced to capitulate and grant their demands for better conditions. It is almost impossible for us to comprehend the savagery of naval discipline, but some indication may be gained from the fact that a common punishment was five hundred lashes, administered on the bare back of the culprit by men in relays, so that the force of the blows would not diminish. When the wretch being punished was nearly beaten to death, he was cut down, restored to health, and then given the remaining lashes. Upon the basis of such atrocities rested the glorious victory of Trafalgar.

The laws. In no other respect was the cruelty of the age as apparent as in its criminal laws. Every class agitated for the death sentence as punishment for any act which injured it. Burke declared that he could obtain the assent of Parliament to any bill imposing the death penalty – about the only type of bills which the Whig minority could expect to pass! Of the two hundred and twenty-three offences for which capital punishment was inflicted, one hundred and fifty-six had actually been so designated during the reigns of the Georges. Furthermore, the classification of capital offences was hopelessly chaotic, so that a poor wretch never knew when he was bringing himself into the shadow of the gallows. If he cut his initials on Westminster Bridge, or otherwise disfigured it, if he shot a rabbit, if he appeared disguised on the public highways, if he stole property valued at five shillings, if he stole a piece of bread from a boat, if he stole anything at all from a bleach-field – for these and many similarly petty offences he was liable to be hanged. Nor did the severity of the sentence act as any great deterrent to convictions. In 1818, there were at one time fifty-eight persons under sentence of death, of whom one was a ten-year old child. In 1776, Charles Wesley noted in his diary, "I preached a condemned sermon to about twenty criminals; and every one of them, I had good grounds to believe, died penitent. Twenty more must die next week."

The prisons. Jailers received no salary. Indeed, they paid as much as forty pounds a year for the privilege of exploiting the prisoners in their charge. Food, bedding, clothing, and accessories of every sort must be purchased by the prisoners from the jailer, at any price he chose to ask. Prisoners who had money were pitilessly robbed. Those who had none were chained at the door of the prison to permit them to beg from passers-by, and were condemned to hopeless slavery to their jailers until the ever-accumulating debts could be paid. Conditions within the jails were miserable. Lord Cockburn's description of Edinburgh's jail, in the famous *Heart of Midlothian*, could be applied with little change to all of them:

> A most atrocious jail it was, the very breath of which almost struck down any stranger who entered its dismal door. It was very small, the entire hole being filled with little dark cells; heavy manacles the only security; airless, waterless, drainless; a living grave. One week of that dirty, fetid, cruel torture-house was as severe punishment than a year of our worst modern prison.

John Howard's researches into prisons all over England, and in Europe, confirmed this picture and, belatedly, led to a prison reform.

Mine labor. The historian Mackenzie has summarized conditions that were typical not only of the mines, but of the new industrial plants: "Women and children worked in coal-pits. They dragged about little waggons by chains fastened round the waist, they crawled like brutes on hands and feet in the darkness of the mine. Children of six were habitually employed. Their hours of labor were fourteen to sixteen daily. The horrors among which they lived induced disease and early death. Law did not seem to reach to the depths of a coal-pit, and the hapless children were often mutilated, and occasionally killed, with perfect impunity by the brutalized miners among whom they labored. There was no machinery to drag the coals to the surface, and women climbed long wooden stairs with baskets of coal upon their backs."

Duelling. Of this practice, it is only necessary to say that lives so valuable to England as those of Pitt, Fox, Castlereagh, Canning, O'Connell and Wellington were, during this period, risked in duels.

Doubtless any period is distinguished by many abuses which are not recognized nor redressed in its time, but which appear monstrous to succeeding generations. The eighteenth century, however, was particularly crass and inhuman in many repects.

It would be easy to interpret the century as a unit – to close our eyes to its complexities, contradictions and growth – to overlook the great diversities among the social strata and occupational classes. But in the last quarter of the century the conventional mold (if it ever really existed) was breaking to pieces. Amid militant literary romanticism, philosophical humanitarianism, and political liberalism – strongly opposed by their contraries of neo-classicism, crass commercialism, and toryism – a new age was struggling to be born. It was a time in which a preponderantly rural population was becoming chiefly urban and industrial; in which a formal and rational religion was being infused with the new enthusiasm of Methodism; in which the old accepted hierarchal structure of society and government was tottering before new conceptions of freedom, equality, and utility. The new and powerful weapon of public opinion was being created by the extension of newspapers and magazines; political parties were beginning to be formed around principles, rather than upon loyalties to dynasties and families. It was a time in which the solid train of English victories, resulting in the creation of an unrivalled world empire under the inspired premiership of the Earl of Chatham, was to be broken, the choicest part of that empire lost, and England to find herself an isolated outcast among the nations of Europe. It was an age in which a new concern for the dignity and worth of the common man was to struggle against the blind retrenchment of a ruling class mad with the fear of French Revolutionism. Philosophy, literature, economic theories, scientific inventions, government, and oratory were joint products and joint producers of the new trends. Looking back upon the period it appears that, far from being static, it was a time of tremendous and most significant change.

But to "look back" upon it is to miss its meaning. The significant question is not, how does the age appear now, with all of the irrelevancies winnowed out, but how did it appear to its own inhabitants? What issues seemed important to them? What problems, perhaps now trivial, formed the passing attractions of their days? What gossip helped form their attitudes toward public men? It is orientation more than historical perspective that brings past epochs back to life. And, for that purpose, more is needed than a reperusal of state documents.

It is necessary, in addition, to travel about England with Fielding's Parson Adams and Tom Jones, to sigh with the sentimental over the plights of Richardson's virtuous (but expedient) Pamela, and listen for the angelic harp-strains from his heaven-rewarded Clarissa Harlowe. Its characteristics are illustrated by Uncle Toby waiting for the birth of Sterne's Tristram Shandy, and in the unfortunate mishaps of the sadistic Smollett's naval characters. In the pages of "Monk" Lewis, Walpole's *Castle of Otranto*, and the grizzly narratives of Ann Radcliffe and the Bronte sisters, lies the captivating horror that enthralled the readers of that age. Crabbe's searing presentation of the lot of the poor must be contrasted with the idyllic interpretation Irving, Cowper, and Goldsmith gave to the same theme. Readers must follow along with Boswell at the heels of the great bear, Dr. Johnson, while he charms and overwhelms his conversational associates and in his talk presents a vivid picture of one phase of the life of the time. They should listen to the malicious gossip of Horace Walpole, the aimless chatter of Fanny Burney, the sophisticated advice of Lord Chesterfield, the pious zeal of John Wesley, and read the intimate letters of Cowper, Gray and Gibbon. Or examine politics through the personal prejudices of Lady Sarah Lennox, William Wilberforce, Lord Holland (the nephew of Fox), the third Duke of Grafton, Lord Sidmouth, Samuel Rogers, Nathaniel William Wraxall, and George the Third. The age is expressed in the humanitarian reforms advocated by Howard, Clarkson, and Wilberforce; economic facts and theories stated by Ricardo, Price, Smith, Young, and Malthus; the philosophy of Hume, Bentham, and Mill. It takes form in the literary criticism of Dr. Johnson on the one hand and William Wordsworth on the other; in political theory, with a long line of controversialists from Hobbe and Locke, through Bolingbroke, Montesquieu, and Rousseau, to Burke and Paine. And finally, from the intermingled impressions of these diverse threads comes the conviction that a new age was being born.

The problems are to determine what effect this convergence of changes had upon the speaking of the orators of that day and to what degree their speeches shaped the course of events. Were Burke, Fox, Sheridan, and Pitt greatly affected, for instance by the industrial revolution? Judging from historical perspective, that appears to have been the great movement of the times. But there is no evidence in Boswell's *Johnson*, nor in the letters of Walpole or Cowper, nor in the poems of Burns or Blake, nor in the speeches of these men or their parliamentary associates, that the movement was of great significance to them. It is the judgment of most historians that the industrial revolution proceeded so quietly and so gradually that men did not realize its importance until long after society had completely changed.

Were these speakers and their associates moved by humanitarian zeal? Only, it may be answered, so far as distant peoples were concerned. The horrors of the African slave trade became real to them, and Burke was aroused by the oppression of the people of India. But they were not real humanitarians. The indignation for the wrongs of India was aroused, at first, by a disappointed and jealous rival of Hastings; and the anti-slavery movement originated outside of Parliament. The evils of the prison system were protested only by John Howard; unemployment and poverty were not considered proper legislative concerns. Burke declared that he "Disliked the cant concerning the Poor. The Poor are not poor, but Men, as we are all born to be. Those who have known luxury, and are reduced, meet with most of my compassion." Sheridan did protest in Parliament against bull-baiting, and against an old (and by that time ignored) law providing that women traitors should be burned. But real social sympathy, and with it legislative responsibility to reform evils, did not become characteristic of politics until well into the next century. Sir Leslie Stephen aptly characterized the ruling class of the time in his description of Edward Gibbon: "A peaceful acquiescence in the established order, not an heroic struggle toward a fuller satisfaction of all human instincts, is his ideal.

Equilibrium, at whatever sacrifice obtained, is the one political good."

Despite the complacency with which the governing minority regarded its position, there was operating at that period the same flux which always affects society. At some periods the flux attains whirlwind proportions, as in France during the Revolution. At others its speed is increased without getting out of control. Such a period as this last was the England of the four decades from 1765 to 1806. In any society there are always stirrings of three diverse currents: distintegration and decay of old institutions, traditions, and habits of mind; a reactionary movement to stem the decay by reversion to the strictest form of the tradition; and an effort to convert the old society into a new, through destruction of the old forms and adoption of new ones. Beneath the surface, these three forces were proceeding with accelerating speed in the England of the latter part of the eighteenth century. They affected all aspects of life, and their ramifications influenced the oratory of the period in many and diverse ways.

Part Two

Their Audience

Chapter 3 – The Parliament – Corrupt

Any speaking is, of course, profoundly affected by the
type of audience which the speakers address. And the term
"audience," used in such a connection, must be broadened
beyond the immediate hearers. It must include all the
groups whom the speakers addressed indirectly (as well as
those addressed directly), for they, too, exercised a considerable influence upon the mode of speaking. In this sense,
the audience of Burke, Fox, Sheridan, and Pitt might truly
be thought of as having been composed of three groups.
These were the members of the House of Commons, whom
they directly addressed; the King, who exercised a large
influence over the members of Parliament; and the general
public, who, for the first time, were becoming articulate and
making public opinion an effective political instrument.
These three bodies might almost be considered as representing, roughly, the three forces operating in the politics
of that day. Certainly the political disintegration showed

itself very plainly in the parliamentary corruption of the time; the King represented militant Tory reactionism; and among the people were commencing to stir the first signs of effective demands for reform.

The first thing to note about Parliament as an oratorical audience is that it did not pretend to represent the people of England. In a population of about 8,000,000, there were only 160,000 voters. Furthermore, it has been estimated that 5,723 voters elected fully half of the members of the House of Commons, and that 364 voters elected one-ninth of the members. Besides the 558 members of Parliament elected to the House of Commons, there were, at the end of the century, 268 peers in the House of Lords. Thus the parliamentary audience of that day was homogeneous. It represented largely one class, and was bound together by common interests and prejudices. It should not, however, be concluded that it was an assembly of polished gentlemen. The contrary was true of many of the members.

The best picture of any situation is likely to be drawn by one who sees it with the fresh interest of a stranger; for he does not omit or blunt details that have been seen so often as to have lost their significance. Thus in the *Travels* of the German student, Carl Philipp Moritz, his description of his first visit to Parliament, in 1782, brings that body almost into the focus of direct observation. Moritz tells of his attempt to get into the galleries, and of being turned away by the tall man dressed in black who guarded the door – until he was bribed (a species of persuasion which was widely used in that time and in those halls.) Since this chapel of St. Stephen's, where the Commons met, was the setting for the speeches to be examined, it may well be observed in the full detail presented by Moritz.

"And thus I now, for the first time," he said, "saw the whole British nation assembled in its representatives, in rather a mean-looking building, that not a little resembles a chapel. The Speaker, an elderly man with an enormous wig, with two knotted kinds of tresses, or curls, behind, in the black cloak, his hat on his head, sat opposite to me on a lofty chair; which was not unlike a small pulpit, save only that in front of it there was no reading desk. Before the Speaker's chair stands a table, which looks like an altar; and at this there sit two men, called clerks, dressed in black, with black cloaks. On the table, by the side of the great parchment acts, lies an huge gilt sceptre, which is always taken away and placed in a conservatory under the table, as soon as ever the Speaker quits the chair. . . .

"All round on the sides of the house under the gallery are benches for the members, covered with green cloth, always one above the other, like our choirs in churches; in order that he who is speaking, may see over those who sit before him. The seats in the gallery are on the same plan. The Members of Parliament keep their hats on, but the spectators in the gallery are uncovered.

"The Members of the House of Commons have nothing particular in their dress; they even come into the house in their great coats, and with boots and spurs. It is not at all uncommon to see a member lying stretched out on one of the benches, while others are debating. Some crack nuts, others eat oranges, or whatever else is in season. There is no end to their going in and out; and as often as any one wishes to go out, he places himself before the Speaker, and makes him his bow, as if, like a school-boy, he asked his tutor's permission.

"Those who speak, seem to deliver themselves with but

little, perhaps not always with even a decorous, gravity. All that is necesary, is to stand up in your place, take off your hat, turn to the Speaker (to whom all the speeches are addressed); to hold your hat and stick in one hand, and with the other hand to make any such motions as you fancy necessary to accompany your speech.

"If it happens, that a member rises, who is but a bad speaker, or if what he says is generally deemed not sufficiently interesting, so much noise is made; and such bursts of laughter are raised, that the member who is speaking can scarcely distinguish his own words. This must needs be a distressing situation; and it seems then to be particularly laughable, when the Speaker in his chair, like a tutor in a school, again and again endeavours to restore order, which he does by calling out *to order, to order*; apparently often without much attention being paid to it.

"On the contrary, when a favourite member, and one who speaks well and to the purpose, rises, the most perfect silence reigns: and his friends and admirers, one after another, make their approbation known by calling out, *hear him*; which is often repeated by the whole house at once; and in this way so much noise is often made that the speaker is frequently interrupted by this same emphatic *hear him*. Notwithstanding which, this calling out is always regarded as a great encouragement; and I have often observed, that one who began with some indiffidence, and even somewhat inauspiciously, has in the end been so animated, that he has spoken with a torrent of eloquence. . . I have sometimes seen some members draw a kind of memorandum out of their pockets, like a candidate who is at a loss in his sermon: this is the only instance in which a member of the British parliament seems to read his speeches."

Moritz went on to say, perhaps with his tongue in his cheek: "I have since been almost every day at the parliament house, and prefer the entertainment I there meet with, to most other amusements." One type of this amusement he describes: "It is quite laughable to see, as one sometimes does, one member speaking, and another accompanying the speech with his action. This I remarked more than once in a worthy old citizen, who was fearful of speaking himself, but when his neighbor spoke, he accompanied every energetic sentence with a suitable gesticulation, by which means, his whole body was sometimes in motion."

To these comments of Moritz we might make one addition and one correction. The Ministers and their supporters sat on one side of the House, — the Opposition on the other, so that each speaker, surrounded by his friends, spoke across the room to his opponents; and the Parliament was decidely not representative of the British nation.

In fact, as we analyze the Parliament to discover the elements in the situation having the most effect on the speeches, we are struck first of all by the decidedly unrepresentative character of the members. First of all, many of them were returned from a "pocket" or "rotten" borough, either their own "property" or that of another person whose political mouthpiece they were. Secondly, regardless of how the members got into Parliament, a great many of them were bribed by the patronage of the Crown, and cast their votes directly as the ministers bade. Many more who were not "placemen" voted unvaryingly with the Ministry in hopes of being appointed to some sinecure; in fact, those members who were incorruptible were regarded as being somewhat odd. It was this handicap of an audience whose votes were bought and paid for in advance that Fox, Burke,

Sheridan and their friends had to face. It is their triumph over this handicap, year after year, that constitutes one of their chief distinctions as statesmen and orators.

The corruption of Parliament consisted, first of all, in strict limitation of the suffrage, and in the "rotten" borough system. In 1793, a petition was presented in the House of Commons on behalf of the Society of the Friends of the People demanding an electoral reform. It was based upon facts that could not be denied. Besides the 35 places in which the elections were a mere form, there were in England 46 in which the voters were not more than 50 in number, 37 more where they were not more than 100, and 26 where they did not exceed 200. Most of these constituencies returned 2 representatives, so that they accounted in all for 249 members of Parliament. In Scotland, there were 30 members for counties with less than 250 electors each, and 15 for districts or boroughs with less than 125. Thus 284 members, or a majority of the House, were elected by what was comparatively a mere handful of the population. But the analysis did not end here. The Friends of the People went on to show that 84 individuals sent 157 men to Parliament by their own immediate authority, and estimated that 150 more were returned chiefly on the recommendation of another 70 patrons. A large proportion of the corrupt majority of the House of Commons consisted, therefore, of the nominees of 154 persons.

The Earl of Lonsdale personally controlled nine seats in the House, which he called his cat-o'-nine tails. The price of these "close" boroughs was high. When the Earl of Chesterfield offered £2,500 for a seat for his son, he was laughed at. In 1793, Sir Phillip Francis informed the House that seats were then selling for £6,000. Two years later, Galton, in Surrey (which returned two members) was auctioned off for £110,000. Robert Walpole made bribery a science, and office an unfailing source of income. For example, he appointed his eldest son auditor of the Exchequer, his next son clerk of the pells, and his third son was made clerk of the estreats while still at Eton, and usher of the Exchequer before he left Cambridge. One nobleman had £8,000 a year in sinecures, and the colonelcies of three regiments. Another, as auditor of the Exchequer (into which he never looked) had £8,000 during peace-times, and £20,000 in time of war. A Scotsman had a captain's commission for his ten-year old son, an income of £3,000 a year, and the reversion of £17,000. An Irish politician was at one and the same time a privy-councillor; reversionary secretary of state; major of the fourth regiment of horse; provost of Trinity College, Dublin; and searcher, packer, and gauger of the port of Strangford!

It is no wonder that Lord Chatham declared in the House of Lords, "If any noble Lord challenge me to assert that there is much corruption in both Houses, I would laugh in his face, and tell him that he knows it as well as I." One member declared openly in the House of Commons, "If I had a son, I would say to him, 'Get into Parliament. Make tiresome speeches. Do not accept the first offer; but wait until you can make great provision for yourself and your family; and then call yourself an independent country gentleman.' " In short, this was "a period when people entered Parliament, not because they were rich, but because they wanted to be rich, and when it was more profitable to be a member of a cabinet than the partner in a brewery."

The corruption, of course, extended downward to include the electors. Thus we find that Sheridan's own note for his election expenses in 1784 shows that he paid 284 burgesses 5£, five shillings each, besides 86£, eleven shillings spent on others of his constituency. His election in 1780 cost him 2,000£. In the hotly disputed campaign in Westminster in 1784, Fox stood on a platform of "Liberty and no backstairs influence." Bribery was freely used to defeat him, and quite possibly in his behalf. A favorite way of bribing was for a supporter of a candidate to tell a voter, "I'll lay you five guineas, and stake the money in your own hands that you will not vote for Fox." Many a "bet" was thus accepted and the vote determined by it.

In that day, bribery and corruption were just as common, and just as open, as log-rolling is in the legislatures of the present. There were many then, and even some later historians, who have defended the "rotten" borough system. "The patron did not expect," wrote Robert H. Murray, in *Edmund Burke, a Biography*, "and certainly did not receive a humiliating dependence on the part of the member of Parliament returned for his close borough. The Patron felt that he was affording an opportunity to a promising young man who might otherwise experience difficulty in finding a seat." That this altruistic motive may have operated occasionally is probably true, but that it was the reason close boroughs were valued at times as high as £55,000 apiece, and commonly for from £2,500 to £6,000 is beyond reasonable belief.

It is true that the close boroughs were the instruments for introducing a remarkable body of talented men into Parliament, including Chatham, Pelham, Percival, Burke, Fox, Pitt, Canning, Wellesley, Plunket, Brougham, Horner, Romilly, Liverpool, Lord John Russell, Hume, Macaulay, and Gladstone. But it also introduced a great number of self-seeking place hunters. These men, at the king's nod, defeated Fox's East India Bill in 1783, Burke's reform bill in 1780, Pitt's long crusade against the slave-trade, and supported the ruinous American war. The system of parliamentary corruption was a deadly canker in British politics, and it resulted in the formation of the hardest of all audiences to address — an audience which could hardly be moved, for it had no will of its own to express. This audience must be kept in mind while examining the long and outwardly ineffective careers of the four speakers under review.

Thus we have a picture of one portion of the total audience which these speakers addressed, their immediate auditors. Upon a slender base of representation, and a still slenderer base of responsibility felt but dimly by the members to their constituents, was the governing body erected.

Why did it not fall in the general revolutionary fervor which marked the end of the century? Two forces, themselves mutually antagonistic, aided in keeping it erect. On the one hand was a strong-willed Tory king, exercising every reactionary weapon in his power to prop up the old structure of privilege and "secret influence." On the other hand was a newly-born public sentiment for reform, which sought to save the governmental structure by converting it into a true representation of the people. These forces of reaction and reform certainly affected the speech and history of that day.

Chapter 4 – The King – Complacent

The period from 1760 to 1770 was one of steady accumulation of power in the hands of the king. The ministry had become powerful during the eighteenth century partly because the Hanover kings were unable to use the English language, and were very largely indifferent to their island possession. It was this situation that made it possible for the conniving Robert Walpole to bring patronage under the control of the ministry, and thus to insure control of Parliament. When George III came to the throne on October 25, 1760, he was determined to reverse the trend of the last two reigns. His guiding motive was to be the instruction of his mother and Lord Bute: "George, be a king."

The chief immediate obstacle in George's path was the sturdy independence of the Elder Pitt. This powerful Prime Minister was a new phenomenon in English politics. Instead of rising by corruption, he had skillfully utilized his own abilities and was bolstered by an immense popularity, won partly through the magnetism of his overpowering personality, and partly by his extraordinary success in extending the bounds of the British Empire. But George could bear no rival near the throne, and (like the later Kaiser Wilhelm II with his problem of how to manage Bismarck) he ousted his minister who had committed the crime of becoming too great a man. Newcastle, a typically corrupt and corruptible politician, was brought back as the head of the Cabinet. Then, to George's disgust, Newcastle employed his excellent technique of bribery to consolidate the power of his own little coterie of Whigs, rather than playing into the hands of his king.

Had George III possessed the instincts of a democrat, or had he sensed the growing undercurrent of demand for popular rights, he might have immortalized himself as the champion of the people against a decayed aristocracy. The more natural course for him, however, was simply to try to outbid Newcastle for the support of a parliamentary majority.

Once this second course had been chosen, George had an uneasy period while he strove to find responsible ministers who would consent to be merely mouthpieces for him. He came to see the great desirability of having the popular Pitt as minister at almost any cost. But, he finally secured him only after the Great Commoner was too ill to assume the cares of office, and too irritable to secure able colleagues. George nevertheless persisted in his purpose, and, by 1770, when he elevated Lord North to the premiership, he had triumphed.

George III can only be rightly interpreted as an anomaly in English history, a king who corruptly but constitutionally stayed the advance of popular sovereignty. For a brief period, he gathered the reins of government rather securely in his own hands. The great battle of the Whig orators was with this ambition of George's. Consequently, an understanding of their task requires a clear conception of his character.

George had been educated for personal rule. To preserve him from the dissipations of his class, he was reared in solitude, and carefully instructed. As a result of his education and his German breeding, he came to the throne, while still a young man, without experience in meeting and handling people. He determined to have his own way. If not brilliant, he at least was stolidly sensible, unlearned in political economy, but possessed of such private virtues as won him the love of his subjects and the amiable title of "Farmer George."

Yet, he was the type of good man who has a profoundly bad effect. Surrounded by men far abler than himself, he was determined to prevent their abilities from interfering with the extension of the royal prerogative. He dipped into a Parliament containing such statesmen as Chatham, Burke, Grattan, Fox, Sheridan, Mansfield, Erskine, Canning, and Grey, and selected for his ministers as choice a lot of mediocrities as ever governed a great nation: Bute North, Grenville, Grafton, Rockingham, Shelburne and Addington. Even the younger Pitt was suffered by him not chiefly on account of his abilities, but as a buffer to keep Fox from power.

George was well qualified to gain public favor when he ascended the throne. He was young, conspicuously moral, the first of his line to be a real Englishman, and proud of it, as he assured his subjects in his first address from the throne. Yet, there were disquieting elements: his ambition, the influence of Lord Bute, and his stubborn self-righteousness. As Sir Nathanial William Wraxall, M. P. – and a good Tory – wrote in his *Historical and Posthumous Memoirs* "In the King's rountenanre a psysiognomist would have distinguished two principal characteristics: firmness, or, as his enemies denominated it, obstinacy, tempered with benignity. The former expression was, however, indisputably more marked and prominent than the latter sentiment. Fox, when addressing the House of Commons, did not hesitate to allude in very intelligible language to his obstinacy."

Another virtue the Tory Wraxall found in George III was his great loyalty to his puppets. "His present majesty," Sir Nathanial noted admiringly, "neither deserted Lord Bute when most unpopular in 1763, nor the Duke of Grafton amidst the tumults of March, 1769, nor Lord North in the more awful riots of June, 1780. As little did he turn his back on Lord George Germain after the defeats of Saratoga or of Yorktown, amidst the disasters of the American war. Far from recurring for support to his ministers, he constantly extended it to them, and never shrunk from personal risk, responsibility, or odium."

In the light of what we know of George, this praise seems particularly inappropriate. We know that his ministers, excepting the two Pitts, and, to an extent, Bute and Rockingham, were mere puppets for his manipulation, and that he absolutely did not tolerate independence of action or policy on their part. The Elder Pitt was minister for only three years at the beginning of George's reign, and was incapacitated by illness during one of them. The younger Pitt was forced to trim his policy considerably to the will of his royal master; and Rockingham and Bute were independent only in a strictly relative sense. Rockingham nominally represented the Whig demand for parliamentary

responsibility, but his two brief and weak ministries were
a series of compromises with George. Bute exercised any
independence only in the sense that he helped to direct
George along the lines of development which he and
George's mother had devised. Surely with a record like
this, the king would have been most contemptible if he
deserted his puppets when they suffered from meekly obeying him. We find that he did not hesitate to use extreme
discourtesy in dismissing North, his most servile instrument
through a period of twelve years, upon the failure of the
American war, which had been instigated and directed almost solely through George's own perversity. We likewise
must marvel at the unprecedented impudence of his dismissal of the coalition ministry of Fox and North, by send-
ing messengers to route them out at midnight, and refusing
to receive the seals of office from them personally. Surely,
then, George's loyalty must be considerably discounted.

His personal courage is beyond dispute. There were several instances of the exceeding coolness of the king under
the various attempts made to assassinate him, and under
several dangerous attacks from mobs. To those who advised
him to use greater precautions in guarding himself, George
replied: "I know that any man in my dominions, who
chooses to sacrifice his own life, may easily take away mine;
but I hope, if any one attempts such an act, he will do it
promptly, and without any circumstances of barbarity!"
After one such attempt on his life, he said, "I hope and
pray that the poor creature who has committed this rash
assault upon me, may enjoy as sound a repose as I trust
that I shall this night!"

This courage of George is of significance, for if he had
been lacking in that respect he certainly would not have

dared to hold out so stubbornly against the inspired attacks of the opposition orators. Especially during the first months of 1784, when the king's government commanded only a minority of the House of Commons, and was again and again overwhelmed by opposition majorities, George held firm and refused to accede to constitutional demands for a change of ministry. One of the astoundings things about the oratory of this period is its persistence in beating up against a seemingly impregnable wall; and the courageous obduracy of George III was one of the chief factors it could not beat down.

The character and extent of the direct parliamentary powers wielded by George, especially during the first two decades after his ascension to the throne, are clearly indicated by the two volumes of his published correspondence with Lord North. A few extracts will serve to show his interest, sagacity, and determination in imposing his will on the legislative body. The spelling and grammar are the King's own:

1. April 25, 1768: "The expulsion of Mr. Wilkes appears to be very essential, and must be effected."

2. February 23, 1772: "I owne myself a sincere friend to our Constitution, both Ecclesiastical and Civil, and as such a great enemy to any innovations, for, in this mixed Government, it is highly necessary to avoid novelties."

3. March 12, 1772: (Regarding the Marriage Bill) "Lord North, --the turn of yesterday's debate is most favorable, as Opposition, or at least the greatest part of it, have been forced to change its ground and admit that there ought to be some regulations made with respect to the marriages of the Royal Family. It is a known maxim in all military operations that when the enemy change positions that is the right moment to push them with vigor: the rule I look upon as not less good in Parliamentary operations: therefore a continuation of the zeal and activity you have shewn in this Bill will carry it through with great eclat."

5. March 9, 1779: "I wish to see the list of defaulters who have
either employments or military governments."

Finally, there is the more serious communication, which
George gave to Lord Temple early in December, 1783, to
be used in defeating Fox's East India Bill in the House
of Lords, and which actually accomplished that purpose.
"His Majesty," declared Fox in his speech denouncing the
secret influence exerted by George, "allowed Lord Temple
to say, that whoever voted for the India Bill were not only
not his friends, but he should consider them as his enemies;
and if these words were not strong enough, Lord Temple
might use whatever words he might deem stronger, or more
to the purpose."

In such letters as these we have direct and indisputable
evidence of the method by which George III manipulated
the patronage of the throne to overturn the constitutional
powers of Parliament. As Fox observed: "Both Houses of
Parliament are . . . reduced, by this unfortunate and wicked
device, to the predicament of a man struggling for his life.
We are robbed of our rights, with a menace of immediate
destruction before our face. From this moment, farewell
to every independent measure! . . . A Parliament thus
fettered and controlled, without spirit and without freedom,
instead of limiting, extends, substantiates, and establishes,
beyond all precedent, latitude, or condition, the prerogatives
of the Crown."

The forces of reaction, then, as represented chiefly by the
King and his Tory following, were fitted with powerful
weapons, which they well knew how to employ. Throughout
this entire period, reactionary policies were successful in the
main. Only underneath were there stirrings of reform,
which occasionally broke out into very effective expression.

However, the reform forces which were to sweep to victory in the next century were already being mobilized. Now was the seed time which made possible the Reform Bill harvest of the 1830's.

Chapter 5 – The People – Restless

Evidence can be found for almost any picture of social conditions in eighteenth century England. Such social and psychological barriers divided the classes that each was chiefly aware of its own existence. The rich, the middle class, and the poor each left records of its own England and its own mode of existence. It would be easy to trace through the entire century and find a pattern of idyllic ease, tranquillity, and content. And the opposite may as readily be done.

Fully expressive of the self-satisfied complacency of the upper classes are the opening sentences from Thomas Wharton's *History of English Poetry,* written near the middle of the century: "In an age advanced to the highest degree of refinement, that species of curiosity commences, which is busied in contemplating the progress of social life, in displaying the gradations of science, and in tracing the transitions from barbarism to civility. . . We look back on the savage condition of our ancestors with the triumph of superiority; we are pleased to mark the steps by which we

38

have been raised from rudeness to elegance; and our reflections on this subject are accompanied with a conscious
pride, arising in great measure from a tacit comparison of
the infinite disproportion between the feeble efforts of remote ages, and our present improvements in knowledge."

It was recognized, of course, that some poverty existed,
but this was treated with patronizing condescension. The
well-fed squire could look at the surrounding poor and
satisfy his sense of social responsibility by declaring, as did
John Pomfret in his poem, "The Choice,"

> And all that objects of true pity were,
> Should be relieved with what my wants could spare.

But England was to have a rude awakening from this
dream of pastoral bliss. Although the effects of the industrial revolution were hardly recognized before the century's end, other forces were converging to plunge the common people of England into deep and degrading poverty.
As though gifted with prophecy, Thomas Gray wrote, in
1757,

> Man's feeble race what ills await:
> Labour, and Penury, the racks of Pain,
> Disease, and Sorrow's weeping train,
> And Death, sad refuge from the storms of Fate!

England was to undergo a drastic, if peaceful, revolution.
The English Squirearchy, which entered the century triumphant, departed from it with wings clipped. Explanations
for these changes are not hard to find.

The continual warfare of the century withdrew many
men from productive pursuits, and thus led to a shortage
of the food supply. This in turn required an increased
efficiency in farming, which expressed itself in an agricultural revolution. From ancient times the yeomen and petty

farmers in England had depended for support partly upon
the common fields, used as pastures for their flocks. Under
the new pressure of need, however, the fields were enclosed
and turned into large farms, operated with new and scientific efficiency. Jethro Tull invented a drill for sowing seed,
and Robert Bakewell revolutionized the art of stock-breed-
ing. Arthur Young carried all over Europe his researches
into better farming methods. The old practice of permitting
fields to lie fallow on alternate years was replaced by a
system of rotation of crops. Farming took on a new interest
and a new prestige under the patronage of such men as
Coke of Norfolk, Arthur Young, and even the King.

But this agricultural revolution was ruinous to the small
farmers, who formed the bulk of the population. Malthus,
in *An Essay on the Principle of Population* (1798), described the effects of the degrading poverty which overtook
the majority of the people: "The sons of tradesmen and
farmers are exhorted not to marry, and generally find it
necessary to comply with this advice, till they are settled in
some business or farm, which may enable them to support a
family. These events may not perhaps occur till they are
far advanced in life. The scarcity of farms is a very general
complaint; and the competition in every kind of business is
so great, that it is not possible that all should be successful."

The annual marriages in England and Wales, he said,
were one to one hundred twenty-three and one-fifth of the
population. The annual average mortality was one in forty-
seven, in the country, and one in twenty-three in the large
towns. In London, one half of the population died before
reaching the age of forty-five. London, he declared, needed
an annual immigration of 10,000 to supply the deficiencies
between the birth rate and the mortality rate. In all of

England, Malthus estimated, there was only three-fourths as much food as the population actually needed. He reached the melancholy conclusion that nothing could be done to help the poor, for if more money were somehow given to them, prices would rise, and they would be no better off. With this conclusion most public men of the day agreed.

Under such conditions, and with the political leaders indifferent to them, the poor began to take matters into their own hands. Crowds of hungry, jobless, hopeless people gathered in the cities – especially in London – and a Fourth Estate, the mob, came into being. The mob first became a political and social power in England in 1768, during the frenzied disputes over the person of John Wilkes, a political adventurer who had been swept into martyrdom by the stupidity of the crown-controlled Parliament in refusing him his duly elected seat. Immoral, unstable, cynical, – Wilkes was a strange figure to become the hero of a nation. But after he had aroused the determined enmity of the throne for an attack upon it in his periodical *North Briton,* and had been outlawed in consequence, all London re-echoed to the cry, "Wilkes and Liberty!" His picture became a favorite sign for taverns; his wrongs became symbolic of the outrages suffered by the poor. They took up his cause with gusto, and stormed the jail in which he was lodged. In that year, 1768, for the first time in English history, the Redcoats fired upon an English mob. Several people were killed, and this "massacre" might well have become as famous as the similar one in Boston two years later, had not the English mob been in its infancy, and public opinion largely unformed.

That the mob spirit had a lusty infancy, at any rate, was attested by Benjamin Franklin, who observed these London riots of 1768, and left a description of them: "Even this capitol is now a daily scene of lawless riot. Mobs patrolling the streets at noonday, some knocking all down that will not roar for Wilkes and liberty; courts of justice afraid to give judgment against him; coal heavers and porters pulling down the houses of coal merchants that refuse to give them more wages; sawyers destroying sawmills; sailors unrigging all the outward-bound ships, and suffering none to sail till merchants agree to raise their pay; watermen destroying private boats and threatening bridges; soldiers firing among the mobs and killing men, women, and children. . . . While I am writing a great mob of coal porters fill the street, carrying a wretch of their business upon poles to be ducked for working at the old wages."

It is of significance that, as Franklin noted, the mob spirit, once fomented, did not confine itself to the Wilkes issue. It went at once to the heart of the question most deeply concerning the people, low wages and insufficient work. The remedy doubtless was crude, but here, in London, in 1768, was commencing the bitter struggle of class against class which the Industrial Revolution was to make the biggest problem England, and the world, for that matter, would have to solve.

The mobs of London grew rapidly in size, frequency of formation, and influence. In 1780, occurred the most vigorous display of mob power with which George's government ever had to deal. It was motivated by a combination of religious bigotry and general dissatisfaction. In 1778, Parliament had passed a law permitting Roman Catholics who "abjured the temporal jurisdiction of the Pope" to purchase and inherit land, and freed their priests from liability to imprisonment. Only a series of riots in Edinburgh and

Glasgow prevented passage of a similar law in Scotland. The protestant bigots in England determined to force a repeal of this law, and for that reason founded the "Protestant Association," under the presidency of Lord George Gordon. On June 2, 1780, Lord George led a mob of 70,000 persons to Parliament, bearing a monster petition demanding the repeal of the act of 1778. Lord George presented the petition in the House of Commons, and, as various members of Parliament spoke against the repeal, he called out their names to the mob below. A scene of terrible confusion ensued, until a kinsman of Lord George threatened to run him through with a sword unless he desisted. The mob then broke loose in uncontrolled violence, and, from June second to seventh, London was literally in the hands of the mob. The house of Lord Mansfield, England's leading jurist, was sacked, and shops were looted. Public men dared not appear without armed guards. Ordinary citizens were force to wear blue cockades and join in the cry, "No Popery!" to protect their lives and property. Municipal officers were afraid to act against so huge a mob, and the government was helpless until George himself called out his personal troops and the militia to quell the riot. About 450 of the rioters were shot down by the soldiers.

This was the most sensational of the riots, but it was far from being the last. Rioting continued in England as the only means by which the disenfranchised could hope to enforce their will, until it culminated in the huge Chartist movement in the nineteenth century.

The emergence of democracy and the accomplishment of real reforms were only possible if this new public restlessness could find effective expression. Mobs, rioting, and crime could not accomplish a reformation, for all of them were clearly anti-social, and as such were put down by force, with the approval of all respectable citizens. No real public opinion, unified, coherent, and forceful, could arise until there were agencies for molding and expressing it. In other words, the awakening consciousness of the common man was dependent upon a correlative development of the newspaper and the public meeting.

The first English journal had come into being as early as the middle of the seventeenth century. Such genteel periodicals as *The Spectator* had become popular during the first half of the eighteenth century. But it was after 1765 that the modern press was born. The great English dailies date from this time. Among them, the *Morning Chronicle* was establihed in 1770; the *Morning Post* in 1772; the *Morning Herald* in 1780. The great London *Times* also was started in that year. In 1777, there were seventeen newspapers published in London, of which seven were dailies. In 1778, the *Sunday Monitor*, the first English Sunday paper, was established. Between 1769 and 1771, seven new magazines began publication in England.

It was, of course, no accident that journalism sprang so quickly into a full birth. There were many contributing causes, but chief among them may be singled out the restlessness of the people due to the shifting basis of their economic life, and the interest in government which inevitably accompanies a time of increased taxation. There was also the desire for news from the battle-fields, and the dramatic qualities in the character of a number of the public men of the day. The excitement aroused by the persecution of John Wilkes illustrates how this interest spread.

Another character, however, was fully as responsible as Wilkes for arousing the wide-spread interest in politics. This was an anonymous letter-writer to Woodfall's *Public Advertiser*, who signed himself "Junius." Whoever he was, he was a consummate master of the art of blistering, stinging political satire. Moreover, he was someone who had access to government secrets, unpublished, and supposedly known only to a very small group of officials. Intense and wide interest was aroused in his letters, partly from the vigor of his style and the directness of his attack upon public men, partly from his love of liberty and his defense of the rights of the people, partly – perhaps largely – from his carefully maintained anonymity.

Two questions were in the minds of the growing numbers who eagerly scanned every issue of the *Public Advertiser* to see if "Junius" had appeared again. Who is the newest victim of his vitriolic pen? And who can "Junius" be? Over fifty public men were suspected of being the author, as the guessing game got well under way. The secret has been kept to this day, although the preponderance of evidence seems to point to Sir Philip Francis, the able but vindictive politician who came back from India to involve Warren Hastings in ruin, and persuaded Burke to undertake the famous impeachment case. Whoever Junius was, he created a tremendous stir and thus helped establish the popularity of the press.

Naturally, as soon as a reading public was formed, powerful interests seized upon the opportunity offered for the spread of propaganda, and did all they could to fan the flame. A strikingly modern instance of the use made of this new influence of the newspapers occurred during the battle between Pitt and Fox, in the first months of 1784, for control of the House of Commons.

"It was the press, to a great extent, which carried Mr. Pitt triumphantly through this struggle. The East India Company felt their existence to be staked on his success, and they spared no efforts or expense to arouse the nation in his behalf. From the day Mr. Fox introduced his bill into the House, a committee of the proprietors sat uninterruptedly at Leaden-hall Street, for many weeks, sounding the alarm through-out the king-dom; and from that time, down to his final defeat in the general elec-tions of 1784, they used every instrument in their power to defeat his designs. Among other things, caricatures were employed with great effect, some of them very ingenious and laughable. One of them, called the triumphant entry of Carlo Kahn, represented Fox in the splendid cos-tume of a Mogul emperor, seated on the body of an elephant, upon which was stuck the queer, fat, good-natured face of Lord North, while Burke strutted in front as a trumpeter with his instrument in full blast, sounding the praises of the Great Man."

Coincidentally with the rise of the press, other agencies were formed for molding and expressing public opinion. In the winter of 1769-1770, public meetings first began to be commonly held. At one meeting in August, 1769, 7,000 persons were present. The "Society of the Supporters of the Bill of Rights" was founded in this same year by Horne Tooke, a radical politician around whom revolved many of the disputes of the time. The "Constitutional Society," the "Whig Club," the "Friends of the People," and the "Lon-don Corresponding Society," all powerful and extensive or-ganizations, followed in close succession. People having any special interests formed themselves together in groups all over England, and commenced to pour petitions in upon Parliament. Inspired first by Clarkson, then by Wilberforce, the people began to take an active interest in abolishing the African slave trade. When Parliament took up the question in 1792, five hundred and seventeen petitions against the trade were laid before it. The outbreak of the French Rev-olution fanned anew the fervor of the public, and led to a new wave of societies. The "Revolution Society" was established in London on November 9, 1789, and Price preached before it his sermon praising the French Revolution, which called forth Burke's famous reply in his *Reflections on the Revolution in France*. Norwich, Manchester and Birmingham soon had very active pro-French clubs. However, the great majority of the people were opposed to Jacobinism, and violent anti-Jacobin riots occurred throughout England. The worst of these occurred in Birmingham, July, 14-17, 1791, when the mob destroyed the laboratory, library, and instruments of the great liberal scientist, Joseph Priestley.

At first Parliament tried to avoid being influenced by these expressions of the popular will. Measures were taken to prevent the direct pressure of public opinion from operating upon the members of Parliament. An old rule that the galleries could be cleared of visitors on the request of any one member was re-invoked and enforced about the time that public opinion was becoming articulate. Also, a series of libel charges was levelled against the authors and printers of pamphlets which the government considered obnoxious. Wilkes was the first to suffer, for his "No. 45," of *The North Briton*. Following thereafter came trials of Woodfall, the Dean of St. Asaph's, John Horne Tooke, Stockdale, Hardy and his associates, Tom Paine, his printer Williams, and many others. The first considerable check was given to this mode of persecution by Fox's libel bill, which was adopted in 1792. During the French Revolution, a whole series of repressive acts, ranging from suspension of the *Habeas Corpus* to a Treason and Sedition Act, were directed against the assembling of subjects, or any criticism of the government.

But between 1769 and the declaration of war in 1793, the popular will became an increasingly effective force in English politics. Wraxall, writing in 1787, declared: "There is still a tribunal in this country, superior to, and independent of a vote of the Commons, or a sentence of the Lords. It is the Tribunal of the People of England, and of Public Opinion: that ultimate and awful jurisdiction to which Junius appealed, and which gave more than one salutary lesson to Ministers and to Parliaments, in the commencement of the present reign." Freemantle, describing conditions in Parliament at the end of the century, declared that "Every member's vote was weighed in the estimation of his colleagues by the degree in which he represented a popular interest." Writing in 1793, Burke asserted that Fox was guilty of stirring up the people without doors to petition against the war. Fox had said, declared Burke, that "without such assistance, little good could be expected from anything he might attempt within the walls of the House of Commons." Burke added that this popular clamor would have such effect that the "crown should not, in that case, have any use of its judgment."

Thus, in brief compass, we see the three chief currents of the years 1765-1806, which mark the period of the influence of Burke, Fox, Sheridan, and Pitt. The power of Parliament was crumbling, owing to its corruption, limited representation, and consequent lack of prestige. It was assailed on the one hand by the reactionary force of the throne, which George III sought by corrupt control to make dominant once again; and on the other by the groping of the people for a power of their own. In the midst of this flux stood the orators, conscious of these forces, yet feeling their significance but dimly. Every oratorical campaign that they waged, almost every speech that they gave, needs to be interpreted in the light of the historical cross-currents here described. Only as their speeches are seen in their proper historical setting, can they be really understood, for even in a political atmosphere that on the one hand a determined king and his appointed ministers endeavored to continue, the voice of a people just becoming articulate must have had its influence. To evaluate the influence of the rising tide of public opinion upon the oratory of the day is difficult, if not impossible, at this distance from the scene of action. The clue to the actual effect lies in the speeches themselves as they appear against the manipulations of politicians, the rapidly growing complexity of the economic and international scene, and the insistently growing demand of the common people to be heard. The lasting place in history of the four great orators of that period, Burke, Fox, Pitt, and Sheridan must depend upon the way in which their public utterances are evaluated against the backdrop of their day by those whose judgment is dulled by the lack of living details, but sharpened by the perspective of time.

Chapter 6 — Bribery and Influence

With Parliament internally corrupt, and externally controlled by the rotten borough system, it would seem that the power of independent action by the members of Parliament was so limited that debate could have little effect in shifting their votes. It has been asserted that the King could, at will, deliver the majority of the House of Commons to a minister of his choice. Horace Walpole, for instance, in commenting on the debate on the Royal Marriage Bill as it came up for a second reading on February 26, 1772, presented an illuminating behind-the-scenes account of Parliamentary deliberation: "The King grew dictatorial, and all his creatures kissed the earth. It was given out that he would take a dissent on this bill as a personal affront — adieu! qualms, fears, and care of posterity. Zeal, and money, and influence of all sorts went to work, and the consequence was a division against Lord Rockingham's question of 90 to 32."

In such a situation, speaking would seem to be a mere formality, and would either be neglected, or indulged for the sole purpose of display. If such were true, the great orators of the period would be mere exhibitionists, playing prettily with words, to amuse their hearers, and heighten their own prestige as entertainers. In any group of speakers, there are likely to be some who do just that. But such is not "great oratory," and if the condition of Parliament reduced speaking to a level of that sort, it is beneath serious notice.

The key to what were the speakers' purposes lies in the speeches themselves. They were not superficial, not "pretty," and, with some exceptions, were not intended for display. Instead, they demonstrate sincerity and power, two qualities closely connected with purposive speaking.

Yet many have asserted that good speaking was not favored by the parliamentary situation of that day, and even that good speaking did not exist. To Alice Drayton Greenwood, for instance, author of *Horace Walpole's World*, the parliamentary discussions were "entertainment," to be sure of a "somewhat intellectual" type. "Debate," in her opinion, "was regarded as the principal purpose for which the House of Commons existed, and the audience became almost as critical as Athenians. To listen to brilliant speakers scoring neat points against each other, pouring out brisk retort and fierce invective, sailing near the wind and skillfully recovering was their delight. No convictions, no feelings, and few interests of any importance were hazarded."

George Macaulay Trevelyan lent his considerable authority to this view, when he characterized the Parliament as "lost to any argument save gold." Likewise we find the Marquis of Lansdowne, formerly Lord Shelburne, saying of Pitt's government, after its overthrow in 1801, " I think we had from the former Ministry too much of eloquence,

and oratory, and all that sort of thing, and I am glad to see
that the two noble lords opposite take quite a different line."
Lord John Russell expressed his belief that Pitt's brilliancy
as an orator "served only to dazzle and mislead." But
without question, these opinions must be classed as eccentric,
biased, or misinformed.

Lord Macaulay, who had much occasion to know, said
that "Parliamentary government is government by speaking. In such a government, the power of speaking is the
most highly prized of all the qualities which a politician
can possess." The Earl of Chesterfield, who made a science
of success, assured his son over and over again that "eloquence alone enables a man to make a figure in Parliament."
The common verdict of historians is that "Parliamentary
oratory was at its zenith" during this period. Lord Holland
found "the talent of speaking" to be "so necessary to a
public man in this country." "Few men acquire much weight
in Parliament," according to Seeley, "who do not at least
occasionally take a share in its discussions." John Wesley
found that speeches and addresses were vital for the success
of Methodism, and William Wilberforce found them essential in the movement for the abolition of the slave trade.
Sheridan, speaking on the Irish Union Bill on January 31,
1799, said: "The whole world knows that never was there
a period when fine speeches more powerfully affected the
public."

It is evident that the oratory of that day must have been
effective, or the orators would have been discouraged from
their long and arduous labors. Sir Joshua Reynolds, the
famous portrait painter of that age, once expressed wonder
to Burke that he should prepare his speeches so carefully,
knowing in advance that the ministry would be able to mar-

shal a subservient majority against him. Burke's reply gives us the best exposition of the actual effect of the speeches of the Opposition. "I shall say in general," Burke observed, "that it is very well worth while for a man to take pains to speak well in Parliament. A man who has vanity speaks to display his talents; and if a man speaks well he gradually establishes a certain reputation and consequence in the general opinion, which sooner or later will have its political reward. Besides, though not one vote is gained, a good speech has its effect. Though an Act of Parliament which has been ably opposed passes into a law, yet in its progress it is modelled, and softened in such a manner that we see plainly the Minister has been told that the members attached to him are so sensible of its injustice or absurdity from what they have heard that it must be altered.

"The House of Commons is a mixed body; I except the minority, which I hold to be pure," he said slyly, "but I take the whole House. It is a mass by no means pure, but neither is it wholly corrupt, though there is a large proportion of corruption in it. There are many members who generally go with the Minister who will not go all lengths. There are many honest well-meaning gentlemen who are in Parliament only to keep up the consequence of their families. Upon most of these a good speech will have influence."

From a survey of all the factors affecting the circumstances of the speaking of that period, the following reasons for the great parliamentary oratory of the time might be summarized:

Freedom of speech. Outside of Parliament the freedom of speech, both spoken and written, was greatly restricted.

The parliamentary debates were not published until after 1771, and then only sketchily. But perhaps for these very reasons, complete freedom of speech was allowed in Parliament. In our own day, it is almost inconceivable that either government or public opinion would permit frenzied denunciations of a war which that government was then waging, unqualified criticism of the methods by which it was conducted, and open rejoicing over the victories of the enemy. Yet this was precisely the course adopted by Burke, Fox, Wilkes, Barre, and, after 1781, by Pitt, during the American war. It was also, in more aggravated degree, the course of Fox, Sheridan, Grey, Tierney, and the other Foxites during the French Revolution.

These instances are mentioned because it is during a war that freedom of speech is most likely to be checked. But other examples of the unparalleled freedom could be cited in the intervals between the wars, and on subjects purely internal. Thus, during the Gordon riots of 1780, Parliament witnessed the curious spectacle of the mad George Gordon actually standing in the doorway of St. Stephens and shouting out to the raging mob below the names of the orators who were denouncing them. Nor was his utterance checked, until his own kinsman undertook to do it. Englishmen have always been jealous of their right to speak as they please, and this right certainly was exercised in the Parliament of that period.

The potential effectiveness of the speeches. There was always the possibility, however remote, that even the corrupt majority might be persuaded to shift. Certainly, this was the hope that underlay the great efforts of Burke, Fox and Sheridan.

Fox expressed this hope even in 1794, when his following was at its lowest ebb. Writing to his nephew on March 9 of that year, he said: "In the House of Commons we are weak in numbers, but not in argument, nor I think in credit, for notwithstanding Pitt's great majorities it is evident that the House is very far from sanguine about the war, if not altogether disgusted with it. Everything we say against it is heard with great attention, and although Pitt has spoken two or three times extremely well, the House does not appear to be responsive to him."

Arguing often in a good cause, with the facts to support them, it seemed incredible to the opposition speakers that the squalid place-holders could close their ears and remain unmoved. Too, there were occasional successes, such as the astounding vote in favor of Dunning's motion, in April, 1780, that the influence of the crown has increased, is increasing, and ought to be diminished; and Fox's success in 1791 in preventing a war with Russia. This possibility of success was greatly increased by the fact that the county members were essential to the support of any government, and it was possible to win them over. They were in Parliament chiefly to continue their family traditions of service, and remained relatively free from corrupt control. True, they were nominally strong supporters of the government, but there were distinct limits to their subservience. It was the sixty-two votes of county members which were chiefly responsible for carrying Dunning's motion.

But aside from actually carrying or defeating measures, there were three types of considerable influence the speeches could and did have. First, there was their effectiveness, as Burke pointed out, in modifying and gently shaping the policies of the hostile ministry. Sometimes this effect lagged

months or even years behind the speech which impelled it,
but the influence was none the less real. Burke's speeches
undoubtedly were effective in modifying Lord North's
American policy, although, in that case, the modifications
came too late. On the issue of abolition of the slave trade,
the steady efforts of the minority finally wore down the
majority's resistance. During the reactionary fever in England while the French Revolution raged, the small band of
Foxites undoubtedly served by their strenuous opposition
to prevent the huge majority from passing even more subversive measures than were actually adopted. In the second
place, even an opposition oratory could initiate and create
policies which eventually were put into effect. Such were
the reform bill of Burke, the libel bill of Fox, and the
Hastings impeachment as engineered by Francis and Burke.
In the third place, the speeches, however, ineffective they
might be on occasion in Parliament, were of incalculable
value in moulding public opinion. They did this not only
through publication of the speeches in whole, or in sketchy
newspaper accounts, but also through the audiences which
filled the galleries of the House, whenever they were not
closed to the public. Thus, despite surface appearances,
the speakers seldom needed to feel that they were speaking
as in a vacuum, or against forces which could not be moved.

The type of discussion. The organization of Parliament
favored, even necessitated, considerable speaking from the
floor. The committee method was not used in that day,
but every motion was debated and passed upon in full session. This placed upon ever member the responsibility of
making up his mind on every act. Of course this responsibility was largely escaped through a blind obedience to the
King. But even so, there was more tendency to listen to

and be swayed by argument than there is in a day when bills come to the House already, in effect, passed or defeated by committee determination. In those days it frequently happened that a new bill would be introduced to the House, debated, and passed, with the members having no oppority to form opinions about it except from the speeches which they heard.

Informative value of the speeches. The speeches were the main source of information for many of the members. Newspapers and magazines were very scarce during the early part of this period, and at their best they did not have nearly the facilities of the press of today for gathering and disseminating political news. Books dealing with the current issues were also lacking, and the only way the average member could learn about the legislation was by listening to the few men who took the trouble to be well informed. Today, a political speaker is hardly able to talk without referring to facts which his audience has already read in the morning newspaper or heard on the radio; then, the speaker was often able to present facts which were hitherto wholly unknown.

The importance of the issues. Favorable subject matter combined with strong feeling always encourages good speaking. That age, as has been pointed out, was one of warfare between liberal and reactionary forces. The Irish problem, religious toleration, wars, reform, all were stirring issues with great emotional appeal. They were problems which stirred speakers and audiences alike, and energized the oratory with a current of strong feeling. In an age of aspiration and trial, great speech is seldom lacking.

The homogeniety of Parliament. The physical parliamentary circumstances were favorable to good speaking.

St. Stephens chapel, where the Commons met, was small.
The members could easily hear and see one another. Moreover, with few exceptions, they came from the same social
class. The nobility was barred from the Commons, and
relegated to the House of Lords. The lower middle class
found no opportunities to enter Parliament. Hence, despite
the bitterness of many of the debates, there was a funda-
mental homogeniety of sentiment throughout the House.
This is strongly evidenced in the friendship which Fox
maintained with the very ministry which he violently attacked, during the American war. Finally, the debates
were commonly held in the evening, when the members
were mellowed with wine, and when experience seems to
demonstrate that good fellowship and sociability run higher
than during the day.

The prestige of oratory. Lastly, as we have seen, parliamentary speakers enjoyed great prestige, and without speaking it was impossible for a public man to gain public recognition. This motive appealed to the vain and the ambitious
alike, and accounts in part for the determination of the
members to speak well.

It would appear, then, that persuasive speaking in the
truest sense was not only possible in the Parliament of that
day, but that it actually did occur. In fact, one cannot help
being impressed by the fact that it occurred in great pro-
fusion. With orators of a later period, one must often be
content to note at most half a dozen great speeches from
each which form a series of peaks marking their careers.
But in this period of forty years, the facts are that Burke
achieved a high oratorical level immediately upon his entry
to Parliament, and continued on it practically until his death.
Fox was only a little slower in attaining his power of speech.

Sheridan spent several years in learning to speak well after he entered Parliament, but continued to deliver great speeches for over twenty years. And Pitt seemed to leap at once to an eminence from which he rarely descended. There were, of course, variations in the excellence of their speech, but it remains true that the strongest evidence of the persuasive effectiveness of the parliamentary oratory of that time is the continuance of great speaking. Had speaking been merely a matter of form, with little effect upon the votes, surely the great persistence, the prolonged efforts and the evident earnestness of these speakers would have failed from lack of motivation.

Part Three

Their Character

Chapter 7 – Genius on Fire

The England which we have just glimpsed was a stage set for turbulent action. Whether it would be melodrama, tragedy, or heroic drama would only be revealed as the characters assumed their roles. The caste was large and impressive. But as the play unfolded, in a melee of ill-defined factions struggling for control, four figures emerged unmistakably as the stars. To name them in the order of their entry, the first was Edmund Burke, a tall, awkward Irishman, who spoke with a brogue, and whose voice was nasalized by frequent head colds. His long nose, thin features, and eye-glasses (which were still an oddity in that day), together with his several parliamentary inquiries, won for him the nickname of "Peter Pry." Next to appear was the barrel-shaped, dark, hairy, bulky Charles James Fox. He would have looked like a Northumbrian squire were it not for the incongruous dress of a French dandy which he affected, and the almost effeminate shriek which his voice became when he was excited, as he often was.

The last two principal actors appeared simultaneously: William Pitt was tall, thin, prim, prudish, cold, repellant, brilliant, heralded as the promising offspring of the famous Earl of Chatham, whose genius had helped to establish the British Empire, and whose eloquence had cowed and humbled the proudest members of Parliament; Richard Brinsley Sheridan was acclaimed as the greatest dramatist of his age, a popular social and literary figure who had yet to prove his right to consideration as a serious man of affairs. In the hard give and take of parliamentary debate, these four proved their pre-eminence, and through the course of an eventful quarter of a century they did much to shape the destiny of England and of the world.

Edmund Burke's reputation, in his own day was a paradox, representing him as at once "the greatest of English orators," and the "dinner-bell of the House." In the diaries and letters of his contemporaries he is presented as one of England's greatest speakers, yet with such an effect that when he arose to speak, the members arose to leave! Erskine said that he sneaked out of the House when Burke gave his great oration on Conciliation with the Colonies, but that he wore the speech to tatters in reading it afterwards. That speech has been read and analyzed as a prime example of genuine oratory ever since. The question is: Has Burke been over-rated as an orator, or have the criticisms been unjust? The best answers are given by his contemporaries, who actually heard him speak.

The Elder Pitt is reported as saying contemptuously in one of his replies to Burke that "he seldom thought it worth his while to interrupt the right honourable gentleman and

call him to order, or indeed to make him any answer, because his speeches, from their extraordinary style and the
peculiarly violent tone of warmth and passion with which
they were generally delivered, seldom failed to give that
impression which those against whom they were directed
wished them to give."

There were many other testimonies to support this estimation of Pitt's. One is from Carl Phillip Moritz, the
young Prussian who visited England in 1782 and heard
the speeches in Parliament by which Fox and Burke justified
their resignations from the Shelburne government.

"Burke," Moritz declared, "now stood up and made a
most elegant though florid speech, in praise of the late
Marquis of Rockingham. As he did not meet with sufficient attention, and heard much talking and many murmurs,
he said, with much vehemence, and a sense of injured merit,
'This is not treatment for so old a Member of Parliament
as I am,' and 'I will be heard!' – On which there was immediately a most profound silence. After he had said much
more in praise of Rockingham, he subjoined, that with regard to General Conway's remaining in the ministry, it reminded him of a fable he had heard in his youth, of a wolf,
who, on having clothed himself as a sheep, was let into the
fold by a lamb; who indeed did say to him, where did you
get those long nails, and those sharp teeth, mamma? But
nevertheless let him in; the consequence of which was, he
murdered the whole flock. Now with respect to General
Conway, it appeared to him, just as though the lamb certainly did perceive the nails and teeth of the wolf, but notwithstanding, was so good-tempered to believe that the wolf
would change his nature, and become a lamb. By this, he
did not mean at all to reflect on Lord Shelburne; only of

this he was certain, that the present administration was a thousand times worse than that under Lord North (who was present.)"

Another contemporary, Adolphus, believed that Burke's powers were at their zenith in 1774, and that then "his exertions were sufficient to influence, in a considerable degree, the politics of the time: but great and admired as they were, the effect they produced was not to be compared with that which resulted from the efforts of the honourable Charles James Fox." Such testimony is enforced by the reactions of two Tory ladies, both unfriendly to Burke, who recorded their feelings as they listened to Burke's great speech of February 19, 1788, pressing the indictment against Warren Hastings.

Hannah More was overcome with indignation: "I was over-persuaded," she said, "to go to the Trial, and heard Burke's famous oration of three hours and a quarter without intermission. Such a splendid and powerful oration I never heard, but it was abusive and vehement beyond all conception. Poor Hastings, sitting by and looking so meek, to hear himself called villain, and cut-throat, etc.! . . . I think I never felt such indignation as when Burke, with Sheridan standing on one side and Fox on the other, said, 'Vice incapacitates a man from all public duty; it withers the powers of his understanding, and makes his mind paralytic.' I looked at his two neighbors and saw that they were quite free from any symptom of palsy."

Fanny Burney's account is more particularized, fairer, and gives us in brief one explanation of the contradictoriness of Burke's reputation. "All that I had heard of his eloquence," she said, "all that I had conceived of his great abilities, was more than answered by his performance. Nervous, clear,

and striking was almost all that he uttered. . . . When he
narrated he was easy, flowing, and natural; when he de-
claimed, energetic, warm, and brilliant. The sentiments he
interspersed were as nobly conceived as they were highly
coloured . . . and the wild and sudden flights of his fancy
bursting forth . . . in language fluent, forcible, and varied,
had a charm for my ear and my attention wholly new and
perfectly irresistible." Later, however, she expanded these
comments, when talking to Burke's friend, Mr. Wyndham:
"When he came to the two narratives; when he related the
particulars of those dreadful murders, he interested, he
engaged, he at last over-powered me; I felt my cause lost.
I could hardly keep my seat. My eyes dreaded a single
glance toward a man so accused as Mr. Hastings; I wanted
to sink on the floor . . . I had no hope he could clear himself; not another wish in his favour remained. But when,
from this narrative, Mr. Burke proceeded to his own comments and declamation – when charges of rapacity, cruelty,
and tyranny were general and made with all the violence of
personal detestation, and continued and aggravated without
any further fact or illustration, then there appeared more
of study than of truth, more of invective than of justice;
so that in a very short time I began to lift up my head, my
seat was no longer uneasy, my eyes were indifferent which
way they looked, or what object caught them; and before
I was aware of the declension of Mr. Burke's powers over
my feelings, I found myself a mere spectator in a public
place, and looking all around it with my opera glass in my
hand!"

It is upon the basis of such evidence as these citations that
one of Burke's warmest modern admirers concluded, "In
the ordinary sense of the term Burke was not an orator."

Another critic comparing Burke and Chatham, wrote: "Chatham supplied his hearers with motives to immediate action. Burke furnished them with reasons for action, which might have little effect upon them at the time, but for which they would be the wiser and better all their lives after." A similar conclusion is reached by Chauncey Goodrich, one of Burke's great admirers: "Mr. Burke has this peculiarity, which distinguishes him from every other writer, that he is almost equally instructive whether he is right or wrong as to the particular point in debate. He may fail to make out his case; opposing considerations may induce us to decide against him; and yet every argument he uses is full of instruction; it contains great truths, which, if they do not turn the scale here, may do it elsewhere; so that he whose mind is filled with the maxims of Burke has within him not only one of the finest incentives of genius, but a fountain of the richest thought, which may flow forth through a thousand channels in all the efforts of his own intellect, to whatever subject those efforts may be directed."

There may be something to the view that Burke spoke to posterity rather than to his immediate auditors; and that the great moral principles which he expounded are of more importance than the particular issues upon which he spoke. But if critics are right in considering him one of seven of the world's greatest orators, while admitting that his auditors remained unmoved, then surely the definition of oratory needs revision. It is too much to insist that an orator, to be great, must be always successful. To do so would be to reject Demosthenes, among the ancients, and such orators as Calhoun, William Jennings Bryan, and Woodrow Wilson among American speakers. But it would seem inconceivable that there might be a great speaker who did not interest and

move his audience, however they might be decided by other
factors to vote upon the subject of the discussion.

Was Burke lacking in the power that moves? On the
contrary, in his great speeches on American Taxation, On
Economic Reform and in the Hastings trial, he was able
powerfully and continuously to affect his audiences. Yet, it
is significant of the need of a re-interpretative study that
such a careful student of the time as Lecky could deliver
the following reasoned judgment of Burke's final position
as an orator. Lecky concluded: "He spoke too often, too
vehemently, and much too long; and his eloquence, though
in the highest degree intellectual, powerful, various, and
original, was not well adapted to a popular audience. He
had little or nothing of that fire and majesty of declamation
with which Chatham thrilled his hearers, and often almost
overawed opposition; and as a parliamentary debater he was
far inferior to Charles Fox. . . . He far surpassed every
other speaker in the copiousness and correctness of his dic-
tion, in the range of knowledge he brought to bear on every
subject of debate, in the richness and variety of his imagination, in the gorgeous beauty of his descriptive passages,
in the depth of the philosophic reflections and the felicity
of the personal sketches which he delighted in scattering
over his speeches. But these gifts were frequently marred
by a strange want of judgment, measure, and self-control.
His speeches were full of episodes and digressions, of excessive ornamentation and illustration, of dissertations on
general principles of politics, which were invaluable in
themselves, but very unpalatable to a tired or excited House
waiting eagerly for a division."

Any explanation of this paradox of Burke's reputation
must be wrong that does not take into account the element

of time. Burke entered Parliament in 1765, when he became at once exceedingly popular and influential. As years
passed, both his popularity and his influence waned. There
never was a time, it is true, when he was not handicapped
by serious errors of judgment, nor did his influence ever
sink so low that it could not rise again, as it did most notably
in the several years before his death. Burke's life as an
orator should be divided into two periods on the basis of his
personality and popular appeal, and into three periods on
the basis of his influence in Parliament.

From 1765 till 1782 he was continually in the ascendant,
had a large personal following, was the central influence
among the Rockingham Whigs, and was generally heard
with eager attention when he spoke to the House. But in
1782, when Rockingham became Prime Minister, and the
long struggle of the Whigs met with success, Burke was
not admitted to the cabinet. Partly the reason was his
humble birth and lack of family connections, partly his
personal austerity, which failed to make political friends,
partly his irritability, which was even then becoming evident. At any rate, Burke was disappointed by this slight.

Shortly thereafter other blows fell upon him in rapid
succession. Within three months of taking office, Burke's
patron, the Marquis of Rockingham, died; along with Fox,
Burke at once resigned from the government, and went
back into opposition. When, early in 1783, the Fox-North
coalition overcame Shelburne, and assumed the government,
Burke was again excluded from the cabinet. Later that year
his magnificent effort on behalf of the East India bill failed.
Again he was forced from office, and in the elections which
ensued, he saw his party stripped of its power. Three years
previously he had lost his right to represent the independent

constituency of Bristol and had become the representative
of a pocket borough. Now, in 1784, he returned to a Parliament filled with arrogant young Tories, bent upon hum-
bling him. One of them, a Mr. Rolle, reports Lord Russell,
"Showed his zeal by interrupting and coughing down Mr.
Burke." This was a type of political service which other
Tories were quick to ape. "On one occasion [Burke] having
risen to speak with several documents in his hards, a plain
county member presumed to inquire if the honourable gentleman meant to read his large bundle of papers, and to
bore the House with one of his long speeches into the bargain. Never was the fable of the lion put to flight by the
braying of an ass more completely realized: bursting with
rage, yet incapable of uttering a word, Burke strode across
the floor, and positively rushed out of the house."

Under this accumulation of misfortunes, and this kind of
treatment, Burke's temper became completely unrestrained.
During the short-lived coalition, Burke on one occasion
arose to reply to some criticisms made on his conduct of the
office of Paymaster of the Forces. Fox and Sheridan sitting
on either side of him, and sensing the rage with which he
was about to burst forth, grasped him by his coat-tails and
pulled him back into his seat by main force. During his
diatribes on Hastings, and in the Regency debates, it would
have been much better could Burke have been held in his
seat continually. As early as 1781, Horace Walpole, never
friendly towards Burke, wrote, "He was now grown so
heated, and uttered such rhapsodies, that he was generally
very ill heard." In a letter to Fitzpatrick, Sheridan gave
his impressions of Burke's speech on Alderman Sawbridge's
motion for shortening the duration of Parliament: "On
Friday last, Burke acquitted himself with the most mag-

nanimous indiscretions, attacked Mr. W. Pitt in a scream
of passion, and swore Parliament was and always had been
precisely what it ought to be, and that all people who
thought of reforming it wanted to overturn the constitution." Again, in his *Last Journals*, dated April, 1783, Walpole said, "At the end of this month and the beginning of
the next, Burke ran into the wildest intemperance in his
speeches. On the bill for a loan to the East India Company,
he ranted outrageously and most indecently against Governor Hastings, which drew on him severe reprimands from
Governor Johnston and in the public prints; and, in May,
he was no less extravagant in his own defense. . . . In fact
for the last two winters so intemperate had been Burke's
behaviour, that many thought his intellects disordered." Sir
Richard Hill bluntly told the House that he believed Burke
to be insane, and many other members agreed with him.

In 1790, with his publication of *Reflections on the Revolution in France*, Burke began a new period of growing influence, in which he helped to sweep England into war
with France, and in which he led the Old Whigs over to
the support of Pitt, and won a large pension for himself.
But this success did not lessen his acrimony. In the heat of
debate on the fourth of March, 1790, Burke strode across
the floor from the side of his friends and exclaimed, "I quit
the camp! I quit the camp!" Although Fox, in trying to
stem their quarrel, stood before him convulsed with tears,
and unable to say a word for some moments, Burke would
not be reconciled. Shortly thereafter, his extravagence manifested itself when he dramatically drew a dagger from his
coat, threw it on the floor, and exclaimed that that was what
the members might expect from France. Sheridan pierced
this rhetorical bubble by saying, in a loud whisper, "The

gentleman has brought us the knife, but where is the fork!"

Curwen related that as he was waiting for his carriage at the doors of Parliament one rainy night, Burke came up and asked if he might ride home with him. Curwen continued, relating the story in his *Travels in Ireland,* "I could not refuse, though I felt a reluctance in complying. As soon as the carriage door was shut, he complimented me on being no friend to the revolutionary doctrines of the French, on which he spoke with great warmth for a few minutes, when he paused to afford me an opportunity of approving the view he had taken of those measures in the house. Former experience had taught me the consequences of differing from his opinions, yet, at the moment, I could not help feeling disinclined to disguise my sentiments. Mr. Burke, catching hold of the check-string, furiously exclaimed, "You are one of these people,—set me down!' With some difficulty I restrained him; we had then reached Charing-cross — a silence ensued, which was preserved till we reached his house in Gerrard street, when he hurried out of the carriage without speaking, and thus our intercourse ended."

Burke himself told of the extreme disquietude with which he was troubled during those days of revolutionary upset. In a letter believed to have been written in March, 1795, he said: "My heart is sick; my stomach turns; my head grows dizzy. The world seems to me to reel and stagger. The crimes of Democracy and the madness and folly of Aristocracy alike frighten and confound me. The only refuge is in God, who see thro' all these mazes."

From this hasty survey it appears that the riddle of Burke is clearer if his life is analyzed by periods. Obviously, the great orator belongs chiefly to the time before 1783. It was in 1782 that his one great legislative achievement, the pas-

sage of his bill for economical reform, was effected. Earlier
than that, his influence upon legislation was slight, due to
the strength of corrupt influence, but his appeal to public
opinion in the formation of a national sentiment against the
American war was strong. After that time, he became so
intemperate that his effectiveness was greatly lessened.
Even his greatest heights of eloquence in the Hastings trial
were heavily discounted, as was indicated in Fanny Burney's
account, by the invective and personal passion which accompanied them. In 1790, when his influence mounted
again to its greatest heights, his power came through his
pen, not through his speeches.

There were, however, a number of factors which were
relatively constant that interfered with his effectiveness as
a persuasive speaker, as judged in terms of the particular
audience which he addressed. Seven of these may be isolated for particular mention:

In the first place, he was imbued with a tremendous natural confidence in his own powers, which led him unhesi-
tatingly to follow the dictates of his judgment when it led
him against public opinion. This confidence is best expressed
in the speech which he delivered to his Bristol constituency,
following his election in 1774. The chief point of his
speech was that he would follow his own judgment rather
than obeying their will. Putting the case, hypothetically, in
the third person, Burke told the electors that "his unbiased
opinion, his mature judgment, his enlightened conscience,
he ought not to sacrifice to you; to any man, or to any set of
men living. These he does not derive from your pleasure;
no, nor from the law and the constitution. They are a trust
from Providence, for the abuse of which he is deeply an-
swerable. Your representative owes you, not his industry

only, but his judgment; and he betrays, instead of serving you if he sacrifices it to your opinion." These were brave words, and the application of them led Burke solidly to oppose his constituents in their views on the American war, and on the Irish question. In the next election, they cost him his Bristol seat.

Further, this sense of a high moral duty to use his own intelligence to the best of his ability led Burke to champion a series of unpopular causes: Catholic emancipation, reform of the East India Company, strict limitation of the suffrage, and conciliation with the colonies. "I know the map of England as well as the noble lord, or as any other person," Burke said once, "and I know that the way I take is not the road to preferment." Unfortunately for Burke, politics is the science of the second-best; the successful stateman is he who is willing to compromise, to accept what he can get, even though it is far below his ideal of what ought to be done. Because he would not accept this principle, Burke failed much more often than he succeeded in his own day; but for that very reason, his speeches are rightly considered as mines of moral philosophy today.

Paradoxically, self-depreciation ranks with over-confidence as another cause for Burke's ineffectiveness. Like many other supremely confident people, he sought to express a fitting sense of modesty, and did it very awkwardly. "Conscious of my own natural imbecility," he told the House in 1771, "I endeavour to get knowledge wherever I can." Concluding his assertion to the Bristol electors that he should depend upon his, not their, judgment, he said, "I know my inability." Introducing his speech on Conciliation, he told the House, "No man was indeed ever better disposed, or worse qualified, for such an undertaking, than myself." The most prestige he felt entitled to claim when he launched into his discussion of Fox's East India Bill is that he "has supplied a mediocrity of talents by the extreme of diligence." This deprecation he carried over into the party conferences, where he was accustomed to say, "Let us defer to the superior judgment of Mr. Fox." If England accepted Lord Chatham's and the Younger Pitt's high estimates of their own abilities, it is no less true that Burke's habit of ostentatious self-deprecation proved a serious handicap in maintaining his prestige.

His very genius proved to be yet another handicap. He was too intellectual, too profuse with the magnificence of his imagery, for the simple-minded, drink-befuddled squires who formed the largest part of his audience. Lord Chesterfield wrote to his son, warning him against this very danger; ". . . to please an audience, as a speaker, one must not overvalue it. When I first came into the House of Commons, I respected that assembly as a venerable one; and felt a certain awe upon me; but, upon better acquaintance, that awe soon vanished; and I discovered that, of the five hundred and sixty, not above thirty could understand reason, and that all the rest were *people;* that those thirty only required flowing and harmonious periods, whether they conveyed any meaning or not, having ears to hear, but not sense enough to judge."

The Irish orator, Henry Flood, after listening to Burke speak on the American war, wrote to Charlemont: "His performance was the best I have heard from him in the whole winter. He is always brilliant to an uncommon degree, and yet I believe it would be better if he were less so. I don't mean to join with the cry which will always run against shining parts, when I say that I sincerely think it

interrupts him so much in argument that the House are
never sensible that he argues as well as he does. Fox gives
a strong proof of this, for he makes use of Burke's speech
as a repertory, and by stating crabbedly two or three of those
ideas which Burke has buried under flowers, he is thought
almost always to have had more argument."

This difference between Fox and Burke is strikingly
illustrated in a comparison of their speeches on Fox's East
India Bill. Burke's runs to nearly a hundred closely printed
pages, in which great masses of proof are loaded upon a
simple framework in such a manner as wholly to conceal
the central thread of argument from the auditor. Fox's
speech is barely a third as long, and many of his arguments
are supported with scarcely any proof. Yet, for that very
reason they stand out and are impressive. Quite incorrectly,
a careless reader, and almost certainly an auditor, of one of
Burke's longer speeches must sometimes feel that he is
trying to evade a point, when what he is really doing is
smothering it with excess proof. Burke's speeches might
be compared to the Rocky Mountain Range---a great body
of intellectual achievement, but of such uniform height
that the peaks, by contrast, are less impressive. Such speeches
as those of Fox, however, are like Mount Washington, of
less height, yet more impressive because standing isolated.

Uncommunicativeness was also one of Burke's faults.
Doubtless, it arose in part from his intellectual incompati-
bility with most of the members of Parliament. Lecky
thought he discovered another reason, in Burke's age at
the time he entered Parliament. "He was too old and too
rigid to catch its tone, and he never acquired that subtle
instinct or tact which enables some speakers to follow its
fleeting moods and to strike with unfailing accuracy the

precise key which is most in harmony with its prevailing temper." Some doubt of Lecky's correctness is cast by the fact that Burke was most communicative during his earlier years in Parliament, speaking on the colonies, and on his bill for Economic Reform. But whatever the reason may have been, the fact of his uncommunicativeness, in general, is well attested. Thus Lord Liverpool wrote to Croker, "I remember hearing Lord Thurlow say of him and Fox, that the difference between them during the American controversy was that Fox always spoke to the House, and Burke spoke as if he were speaking to himself." Lord Brougham, in *Historical Sketches,* wrote: "In fact, he was deficient in judgment; he regarded not the degree of interest felt by his audience in the topics which deeply occupied himself; and seldom knew when he had said enough on those which affected them as well as him." Such degree of truth as there is in this criticism is a serious charge against Burke's effectiveness as a practical orator.

Another of Burke's handicaps was the suspicion which attended him throughout his political life that he was susceptible to corruption. In the light of his long career of political self-sacrifice, and especially in view of the lack of positive evidence of corruption, these suspicions must be held to be historically discredited. But insofar as his persuasive effectiveness is concerned, the mere fact that the suspicion existed, and that it helped to destroy confidence in him, is of considerable importance. At the age of thirty-five, Burke was very largely a failure, financially, and judged in terms of achievement. In that year, he was introduced to Rockingham, who sensed his usefulness, and made him his private secretary. Rockingham also secured his entry into Parliament. Unaccountably, Burke at once

commenced a series of expenditures consonant with the resources of a wealthy man. A member of Parliament then
received no pay, but had to maintain an expensive establishment in keeping with the dignity of his position. Burke
went further, and expressed his innate generosity by providing Barry, the painter, with sufficient funds to study in
the great picture galleries of Europe, and at Rome. Furthermore, in 1789, he purchased an estate of six hundred
acres, comprising the old home of the poet Waller, at
Beaconsfield, for a sum supposed to have been 20,000
pounds. Besides this cost, the annual upkeep of Beaconsfield was 2,500 pounds, and the income was less than a fifth
of that sum.

It is no wonder that a charge "was current at the time"
that Burke gambled furiously in East India Stock—especially since his brother Richard, his friend William Burke, and
his political patron Lord Verney were all heavy speculators
in that commodity. His brother was also condemned in court
for dishonest land-jobbing in the West Indies, and Burke
himself was accused "in the gossip of the day" of similar
practices in St. Vincents. None of Burke's biographers has
managed to unwind completely the tangled threads of his
financial transactions to their eventual source. But, it is
known now that he purchased Beaconsfield with £2,000 inherited from his elder brother Garret; a £14,000 mortgage
which remained outstanding until his widow sold the property in 1812; and £6,000 advanced to him by Rockingham.
What is inexplicable is why Burke should feel able to com-
mence such a scale of living when his sole visible income was
a pittance received for his work on the *Annual Register*.

Nor did the financial tangle end with the purchase of Beaconsfield. In 1771 Burke accepted the post of general agent

for the Colony of New York, at a salary of £700, a fact
which undermined some of the credence that otherwise
would probably have been given to his claims of total disinterestedness in his speeches on American Taxation, and Conciliation. Before Rockingham's death, Burke borrowed a total of £30,000 from him, which that nobleman wrote off in
his will. Beyond question, Burke earned the money honor-
ably with his political services, but to the gossips of the day
there was strong question of the disinterestedness of services
which were so well paid. Burke's advocacy of his reform bill,
destroying as it did so many sinecures and pensions, aroused
strong opposition to him, without giving him a reputation
for political honesty. Horace Walpole noted maliciously that
Burke had refrained from eliminating the sinecure office of
Clerk of the Pells, because he had intended that his son
should have it. In 1783 Lord Verney stirred up a scandal by
suing Burke for the sum of £6,000 which he claimed to have
lent him. Burke denied the loan, and the suit was dismissed.
But the case was not forgotten.

To cap his career, Burke, in 1795, after he had destroyed
the Whig party by leading a portion of it over to Pitt,
accepted a pension of £3,700. It aroused a storm of resentment among the Foxite Whigs. The young Duke of Bedford
commented caustically on the spectacle of a "reformer" accepting a huge pension for his "patriotic" services. This drew
forth Burke's noble defence of his whole political career in
his *Letter to a Noble Lord*, commencing with a painful reference to "that hunt of obloquy which has ever pursued me
with a full cry through life."

Throughout all of these transactions it is highly improb-
able that Burke was ever actually guilty of dishonorable
practices, and it is certain that he was not nearly so culpable

as were many, or most, of the members of Parliament of that
day. But the fact remains that he was a particular object of
attack, probably because his career was that of a reformer;
the public delighted then as now in finding flaws in the right-
eous. What is beyond question is the fact that Burke's effectiveness as a persuasive speaker in Parliament was greatly
lessened by rumors and gossip about his financial affairs.

Vilifications of Burke's character were also a positive handicap to his political success. Any politician must expect to be
the object of considerable slander, and it was even more freely dispersed in that day than now. The Whigs, being in the
minority, and sponsoring many unpopular causes, were more
violently abused than the Tories, and Burke did not escape.
In view of the personal vituperation which he poured upon
Lord North, Hastings, and the French Revolutionists, he
could hardly have expected to be spared. In the cartoons of
the day on the long drawn-out Hastings trial, Burke was
commonly represented as Peter Pry, one who delighted in
stirring up filth. He was regarded much as were the muck-
rakers in America at the beginning of the present century.
The usual quota of scandal was invented about him, and
circulated in "whispering campaigns." Only occasionally did
it achieve such permanent form as to come down to the present, but its nature is indicated by the reviewer who inter-
viewed Adam Smith in 1780 to get his opinion on certain famous men of the day. In the course of his interview he mentioned "a story about Burke seducing a young lady," which
Smith assured him was pure fabrication. Three years later,
Burke's intimate friend and warm admirer, Windham,
wrote in his diary that Burke "was a man decried, persecuted,
and proscribed, not being much valued even by his own
party, and by half the nation considered as little better than

an ingenious madman." One taint which clung to him to his great political disadvantage was the belief that he was nothing but an Irish adventurer, without family or property, merely seeking office for what he could get out of it. This feeling was heightened by Burke's generous attempts to secure offices for his friends, and pensions or other favors for artists and men of letters who applied to him for help.

Finally, Burke's personal unattractiveness and irritability contributed to prevent his effectiveness in Parliament. This side of his personality has been sufficiently commented upon. How great a handicap it proved to be may be gathered from a comment made years later by Shelburne, then Lord Lansdowne. When he was asked why Burke had never been admitted to the Whig cabinet, he exclaimed, "Burke! he was so violent, so overbearing, so arrogant, so intractable, that to have got on with him in a cabinet would have been utterly and absolutely impossible."

The conclusion, based upon these facts, must be that Burke did not excel as a persuasive speaker. There was point to Sheridan's remark that "in his day he (Burke) was not accounted either the first or second speaker." As literary masterpieces Burke's speeches remain unrivaled, but for practical effectiveness in the give and take of debate, they were excelled by many of his contemporaries.

Chapter 8 —— *Disheveled Advocate*

Fox has always been regarded as pre-eminently a debater. Just as Burke was a master of style, but comparatively weak in persuasion, Fox was careless of his tyle, and concentrated all of his efforts upon the immediate task of moving his audience. Hence, his greatness as an orator depends primarily upon his effectiveness in debate. The question is, then, how persuasive was he? Judged in terms of his tangible achievements, his success was considerable, but not complete. He became the undisputed leader of the Whig party upon Rockingham's death in 1782, and during the next twenty years conducted one of the most vigorous opposition campaigns that England has ever known. He helped to create sentiment against the American war; he defeated Pitt's petty attack upon him through the Westminster Scrutiny; he succeeded in amending Pitt's Irish commercial treaty considerably, and lent his prestige to aid its defeat in the Irish Parliament. He prevented an ill-considered war with Russia in 1791, contributed greatly to freedom of the press by passage of his Libel Act, and won the high respect of historians for his diplomatic ability during his several short terms as Secretary of State for Foreign Affairs. At the same time, he held together a vigorous Whig minority during the dark and reactionary days of the French Revolution, when English liberties reached their lowest ebb since the days of the Stuarts. He prepared the way for the abolition of the slave trade. Finally, through his liberalizing influence and the power of his personality, he originated the great Liberal Party, which renovated and reformed English politics during the nineteenth century. These achievements are solid and substantial. Considered in the light of the handicaps which he had to overcome—his early reactionary principles, the unsavory reputation of his father, the determined enmity of the king, his impulsive hastiness, his own private irregularities, his party views and connections—his persuasive ability must be ranked all the higher.

Nevertheless, his admirers cannot blink the fact that Fox devoted his life to politics, and that he failed to become the directing force of the government. His great abilities were never fully utilized. Pitt succeeded in a twenty-five year contest in keeping him from office. His successes were considerable, but they fell short of being success itself. The question, then, of whether Fox actually was an effective persuasive speaker, must be raised. The evidence constituting the answer may be briefly reviewed.

Speaking of his change of party in 1774, Cunningham says, "before he was twenty-four years old, he was by much the most able support the minister [Lord North] had in the course of a whole session, and within a year after, one of his most powerful and dangerous antagonists."

Fox's nephew, Lord Holland, has preserved an unusual bit of evidence of the attraction which he exercised over his audience even earlier: "I have in my possession a singular

proof of the figure and impression Mr. Fox made on his
first appearance as an orator. A young artist, and, I believe,
a reporter of debates, a Mr. Surtees, of Maniforth, in the
county of Durham, happened to be in the gallery when he
first spoke. At that period no stranger was allowed to take
notes, or take any paper or notebook into the gallery for
that purpose. But this gentleman, struck with the appearance of the youthful orator, tore off part of his shirt, and
sketched on it, with a pencil or burnt stick, a likeness of
him, which he afterwards tried to finish at his lodgings, and
which, owing to the care of Mr. Sharpe and kindness of Mr.
Fletcher, is still preserved in my possession at Holland
House, retaining many traits of resemblance to the dark,
intelligent, and animated features of Mr. Fox."

Henry Grattan, the Irish orator, also bore witness to Fox's
great power at this early period. Many years later, in answer to the question, "Who was the best speaker you ever
heard?" he replied, "Fox, during the American War—Fox
in his best days; about the year 1779." If that were indeed
Fox's best period, his declension must have been very slow.
Moritz, visiting Parliament in 1782, was struck by Fox far
more than by the other speakers. On one occasion the galleries were crowded by eleven o'clock, because Fox was to
speak at four, to assign his reasons for resigning from the
Shelburne cabinet. "Every one was full of expectations,"
Moritz said. "He spoke at first with great vehemence; but it
was observed that he gradually became more and more moderate, and when at length he had vindicated the step he had
taken, and showed it to be, in every point of view, just, wise,
and honourable—he added, with great force and pathos,
'and now I stand here once more, as poor as ever I was.' It
was impossible to hear such a speech and such declarations

unmoved." Moritz heard Fox also on another day, and declared "It is impossible for me to describe, with what fire, and persuasive eloquence he spoke, and how the Speaker in the chair incessantly nodded approbation from beneath his solemn wig; and innumerable voices incessantly called out, *hear him! hear him!* and when there was the least sign that he intended to leave off speaking, they no less vociferously exclaimed, *go on;* and so he continued to speak in this manner for nearly two hours." On this day Fox went from Parliament to a meeting of his constituents at Westminster, and Moritz followed him. Fox was "received with an universal shout of joy," and "the people took it into their heads to hear him speak, and every one called out *Fox! Fox!* I know not why," Moritz confessed; "but I seemed to catch some of the spirit of the place and time; and so I also bawled, *Fox! Fox!* and he was obliged to come forward and speak, for no other reason that I could find, but that the people wished to hear him speak." The interest of the audience on this occasion left nothing to be desired. "Even little boys clambered up and hung on the rails and on the lamp-posts; and as if the speeches had also been addressed to them, they too listened with the utmost attention; and they too testified their approbation of it, by joining lustily in the three cheers, and waving their hats."

In the following year Pitt tried to draw Fox back into the Shelburne government, and Dundas testified that "He [Pitt] has a high opinion of Fox's abilities, and had always wished to have him in the Government, because he thought it impossible to conduct great and difficult affairs with such abilities to criticize them." In 1787, watching the battle between Fox and Pitt, Wraxall wrote of Fox, "Possessing powers of eloquence less copious and brilliant, but per-

haps more solid and logical than those of Mr. Pitt, he is
equally form'd to captivate, to convince, and to subdue." This
is a striking concession from a Tory foe. Several years later,
in 1794, after the wreck of the Whig party, Fox himself
bears witness to the continued power of his speech, in a number of letters to his nephew. Thus on June 23, he wrote:
"We have had warm and good debates in Parliament, in
which if my partiality does not deceive me, our advantage
in speaking has been as great as that of the enemy in voting, especially upon the suspension of the Habeas Corpus
(on May 16), and on my motion for peace (on May 30)."

These citations showing his effectiveness in moving his
audience are amply supported by the judgment of historians.
Lord John Russell in considering why Fox supplanted
Burke as leader of the Whigs, wrote, "It has been said that
the birth and connections of Mr. Fox determined in his favour the question of leadership; but the fact is, that while
Mr. Burke was the greater philosopher, and the more profound reasoner on general principles of government, Mr.
Fox had far more readiness in debate, a more popular style
of eloquence, and more judgment in the practical conduct of
affairs." Lecky asserted of Fox that "That great master of
persuasive reasoning never failed to make every sentence tell
upon his hearers, to employ precisely and invariably the kind
of arguments that were most level with their understandings, to subordinate every other consideration to the single
end of convincing and impressing those who were before
him." Mabel Platz was but stating the universal judgment
when she wrote, "for a union of oratorical and emotional
power with debating ability, Fox has never been rivalled."

These conclusions are denied in an anonymous review of
Fox's "History of the Early Part of the Reign of James

II," which appeared in the *Eclectic Review,* for 1808. "We have remarked," the reviewer wrote, "on the slight hold which our great orator had on the mind of the nation at large; it was mortifying also to observe, how little ascendancy his prodigious powers maintained over the minds of senators and ministers. It was irksome to witness that air of easy indifference with which his most poignant reproaches were listened to; that readiness of reply to his nervous representations of the calamities or injustice of war; the carelessness often manifested while he was depicting the distresses of the people; and the impudent gaiety and sprightliness with which arrant corruption could show, and defend and applaud itself in his presence. It is not for us to pretend to judge of what materials ministers and senators are composed; but we did often think, that if eloquence of such intensity and so directed, had been corroborated in its impetus by authoritative force which severe virtue can give to the stroke of talent, some of them would have been repressed into a very different kind of feeling and manners from those which we had the mortification to behold; we did think that a man thus armed at once with the spear and aegis, might have caused it to be felt by stress of dire compulsion, 'How awful goodness is'."

"Severe virtue" Fox did, indeed, lack, but as a persuasive speaker he had many compensating virtues of a warmer sort. Five of them merit special consideration. His manner was said to be highly conciliatory. To his critics this indicated obsequity and servility; his friends believed it revealed in realtiy a sincere and deep-seated amiability. Fox seemed formed by nature to be liked. Among his political opponents, Wraxall, Gibbon, North, and many lesser men were his friends and well wishers. One of the strongest bonds which held together the Whig party was the loyalty and affection the members felt for their chief. There is much truth in the judgment that "It was impossible not to love him." In this amiability lay much of his political and persuasive strength.

His family connections also aided him politically. As has been pointed out, Fox's father had a well-earned reputation for corruption and dishonesty which was almost unrivalled even in that day. For this reason, Fox began his political life under a cloud of popular distrust. But when his own exertions proved his honesty, and removed this cloud, he was able to use his family connections to good advantage. The Whig party had become, in the course of the century, little more than an oligarchy of powerful families. Through the efforts of Fox and Burke, and the circumstances of George's reign, it was gradually converted into a party of principles. None the less, aristocracy continued to enjoy such prestige that Fox was always aided by the fact of his descent from Charles II, and his immediate kinship with the Lennoxes and Hollands. He was never considered, as was Burke, an adventurer trying to break into the charmed center of the privileged classes. Whatever the upper classes might detest in Fox, they could not overlook the fact that he was one of them; he belonged.

His freedom from the responsibility of office seems a curious fact to set forth as an additional advantage in debate, since the prime object of his speaking was always to obtain office. Yet it is true that Fox was much more unfettered than Pitt. He could hurl charges and suggest policies with an irresponsibility that would have been denied him had he been in office. The ministry was always fair game for any sort of attack; its policy had to be consistent, but the attackers could be as inconsistent as they pleased. Moreover, the ministers had to be very careful of any proposals they might make, for to propose them was to put them into effect. Fox needed to submit his proposals to only one test; would they sound plausible in debate.* He seldom needed to fear that they would have to undergo the actual test of practice. It has been said that every radical becomes conservative when he enters office; he has to guard his actions and his speech. Conversely, the man out of office can base his attack upon all the might-have-beens and panaceas which his fancy suggests. Also, mistakes of the ministry may be used by the opposition as direct evidence of inefficiency; whereas mistakes of the minority, which do not become laws, are soon forgotten.

As another factor, Fox's inextinguishable energy was one of his striking characteristics, and accounted in large part for his success. During the first decade of his career, Horace Walpole never ceased to wonder at his ability to go direct from gambling hall to Parliament and back to his gambling, with never a cessation of activity. This same energy led him to enter into every important debate, and to spare no pains in his parliamentary battles. Fox, himself, made the almost incredible statement that for five whole sessions only one day passed in which he did not make a speech.

*The Foxite Whigs were guilty of four major inconsistencies, all explained on the basis of partisan strife. They opposed Shelburne's peace treaty with America—which was precisely what they had fought for in Parliament for eight years. They opposed Pitt's East India Bill, which was essentially like Fox's (but Pitt was just as inconsistent in opposing Fox's, then bringing out a similar one). They contended in the debates of 1789 that England and France were natural and perpetual enemies, but maintained after 1790 that they ought to live together in friendship. And, in the Regency debates, they assumed the Tory position of advocating the divine right of kings.

Another personal quality must also be considered. Fox's innate generosity and warmth of heart won admiration and affection for him, even though the public sometimes doubted whether he applied those feelings to his political acts. Typical of the attitude toward Fox is the following sentence from an open letter to him written by Samuel Taylor Coleridge, and published in the *Morning Post*, for November 4, 1802: "Nature appears to me to have distinguished you from other men, not so much by rare and splendid faculties, as by an unusual portion of the good, which in a lesser quantity, belongs to all men." Esme Winfield-Stratford, author of the brilliant *History of British Civilization*, states the view of those who loved Fox for his good qualities, but did not trust him politically. "In the inevitable comparison between the two great rivals, Pitt and Fox, the child of the Romantic spirit will most easily attract sympathy. Fox was so openly lovable, he wore his great heart so visibly on his sleeve, that we are naturally more attracted to him, on first thoughts, than to the icicle statesman, with his nose in the air, who seems above the frailties and sympathies of ordinary mortals."

Over against these five factors which aided Fox in his successes, there must be set the handicaps which kept him from the highest success.

Although he commenced political life as a Tory, Fox almost immediately gained the enmity of the King by strongly opposing the Royal Marriage Bill. This bill was intended to prevent any marriage in the royal family which was not sanctioned by the King. Fox was hereditarily opposed to it; his own cousin, Lady Georgianna Lennox, had attracted the youthful admiration of George when he was Prince of Wales, but their marriage was prevented by his family.

Thus the Royal Marriage Bill seemed particularly obnoxious to Fox, and he opposed it violently. On other occasions, too, he differed from his sovereign, until George conceived a strong personal dislike for him, and finally drove him from the Tory camp. When the American war broke out, Fox denounced it as the King's war, and placed full responsibility for its failures upon George. When the Rockingham Whigs overthrew North's government in 1782, George so hated these associates of Fox that he conducted all negotiations for the new cabinet through Shelburne. Upon Rockingham's death in July, he precipitated Fox's resignation by making Shelburne Prime Minister. After Shelburne was defeated by the Fox-North coalition, George actually threatened to resign his throne and return to Hanover, rather than turn the government over to them. Discretionary counsels prevailed over him, and he presented the seals of office to Fox and North. It was oberved by courtiers, however, that he looked very much like a horse that had already determined to throw its riders. A few months later, after use of illegal means of defeating the coalition in the House of Lords, he sent a messenger to rout Fox and North out at midnight to give them their dismissal. For the rest of his political life, Fox was barred from office by the strong will of George. It was not until after Pitt's death that a new coalition, dubbed by Sheridan "the ministry of all the talents," brought Fox into office again. Whatever his abilities and whatever his influence, Fox was doomed to political ineffectiveness by his enmity with the King. The conflict of their characters perhaps made the impasse inevitable, but it was Fox's greatest misfortune and mistake.

Another handicap to Fox's political effectiveness was his passion for gambling. This passion had been deliberately

implanted in him by his father, and it exceeded all bounds,
even in a gambling age. As a mere youth of sixteen, he con-
tracted gambling debts of £100,000, and this extravagance
continued almost unabated for twenty-five years after his
entry into Parliament. In 1781, his library had to be sold at
auction to pay his most pressing creditors. He was continually hounded by them, yet continually ran up new debts
at the gaming tables. In 1793, his friends banded together
to purchase him an annuity, and this was sufficient to make
him renounce gambling thereafter. But the damage to his
reputation was already done. In a Fast Sermon of 1797,
which was widely circulated, Dr. Price denounced Fox in
terms which were agreed to by many others:

> "Can you imagine that a spendthrift in his own concerns will make
> an economist in managing the concerns of others? that a wild gamester
> will take due care of the state of a kingdom? Treachery, vanity, and
> corruption must be the effects of of dissipation, voluptuousness, and impi-
> ety. These sap the foundations of virtue; they render men necessitous and
> supple, ready at any time to fly to a court in order to repair a shattered
> fortune and procure supplies for prodigality."

Dr. Price was one of the leaders of the English Dissenters, and one of the best refutations of his charges is the fact
that Fox continued to be their ardent champion in Parliament until his death, although they often deserted him.
But, those who wished to disagree with him politically did
not hesitate to use his gambling as a lever with which to
overturn his reputation. The disastrous election of 1784,
in which more than seventy of Fox's followers were defeated, shows how successful they were.

Such a keen observer as Wraxall believed that those first
two factors, his enmity with George III and his gambler's
reputation, were alone sufficient to explain his failures:
"Equal to his antagonist [Pitt], in all the sublime talents

requisite for the government of an empire: superior to him in modern and polite knowledge; in an acquaintance with Europe, its manners, its courts, and its languages; he is his inferior only in one requisite; an opinion of his public principle, generally diffus'd among the people. When to this great and inherent defect, is super-added the unquestionable alienation of his Sovereign, both to his person and his party; we may lament, but cannot be surprised, that abilities so universal and sublime are left unemployed . . . " Horace Walpole preserved a passage in debate which illustrates how Fox's indiscretions were used to destroy his political prestige. In the debate on December 4, 1777, on the Habeas Corpus act, Fox charged Thurlow with a" black act." "Thurlow answered him warmly, and asked if, supposing his character a black one, Fox's was a white one."

Certainly another reason Fox did not succeed more largely was his unwillingness to devote his whole life to politics. Ambition was far from being the ruling motive of his life. He has been described as a votary of pleasure, but this was true only of his youth. It would be much more accurate to describe him as a devotee of fine living. While still an undergraduate at Oxford, he amazed his colleagues with the range and exactness of his knowledge of Greek literature. When a clergyman eminent for his knowledge of Greek tried to prove that a verse in the Iliad was spurious because it contained measures not used by Homer, Fox instantly recited twenty other verses of the same measure. Such was his knowledge of the classics.

He spent the years from 1797 to 1802 in virtual retirement at St. Anne's Hill, occupied with just such studies. He wrote to his nephew, "Oh, how I wish that I could make up my mind to think it right to devote all the remaining part of my life to such subjects, and such only!" For years before this, when he was in the thick of parliamentary battles, his real desires were centered around his home and his books, as a letter dated April 25, 1794, illustrates:

"Here I am passing a most comfortable week of holidays, the weather delicious, and the place looking beautiful beyond description, and the nightingales singing, and Mrs. A. [his wife] as happy as the day is long — all which circumstances enable me to bear public calamities with wonderful philosophy; but yet I cannot help thinking now and then of the dreadful state of things in Europe, and the real danger which exists, in my opinion, of the total extinction of liberty, and possibly of civilization, too, if this war is to go on upon the principles which are held out."

This is evidence that the man whom his enemies pictured as a creature of ruthless ambition, willing to sacrifice his honor and his country for power, was actually happiest in the quiet life of a studious country gentleman. If only one quality were named as essential to success, it might well be the concentration of overwhelming ambition, the centering of all one's efforts around a single goal, and the sacrifice of everything else to its achievement. This is what Pitt did; it is very far from what Fox did. Happiness, rather than ambition, was his guiding star. In early life, he found his satisfaction in activity and excitement, such as that furnished by the gaming table, and the contests in Parliament. After his bitter struggle and defeat in 1783-1784, he gradually came to care less and less for political success. If the question is asked why Fox failed to achieve the highest effectiveness in moving Parliament, the true answer may be discovered in the real satisfaction which he found in his life outside of Parliament, removed from squabbles, responsibilities, partisan strife and cares.

The curtains have been drawn back from his retirement at St. Anne's Hill, by his secretary Mr. Trotter, who gives us a glimpse into the quietude and contentment that Fox so much preferred:

"The domestic life of Mr. Fox was equally regular and agreeable. In summer, he arose betwixt six and seven; in winter before eight. The assiduous care and excellent management of Mrs. Fox rendered his rural mansion the abode of peace, elegance, and order, and had long procured her the gratitude and esteem of those private friends whose visits to Mr. Fox, in his retirement at St. Anne's Hill, made them the witnesses of this amiable woman's exemplary conduct. I confess I carried with me some of the vulgar prejudices respecting this great man. How completely was I undeceived! After breakfast, which took place between eight and nine in the summer, and a little after nine in winter, he usually read some Italian author with Mrs. Fox, and then spent the time preceding dinner in his literary studies, in which the Greek poets bore a principal part. A frugal but plentiful dinner took place at three, or half-past two, in summer, and at four in winter, and a few glasses of wine were followed by coffee. The evening was dedicated to walking and conversation till tea-time, when reading aloud in history commenced, and continued till near ten. A light supper of fruit, pastry, or something very trifling, finished the day; and at half-past ten the family were gone to rest."

Fox's last words were reported to be, "I die happy!" In general he lived happily, not like the "long, lean, hungry men," whose sole ambition is power.

Another cause of his limited success is found in his impulsive, intemperate nature, which made him a poor political party leader. Certainly he was out-maneuvered by Pitt in 1783, when his large majority in the House of Commons gradually crumbled away. Looking back on the results, it is easy to see that Fox was wrong in opposing a dissolution of Parliament and an appeal to the people in 1784. Beyond question he bungled the Regency fight in 1788, when he permitted himself and his party to be forced into the position of practically defending the divine right of kings. In regard to the French Revolution, he never was able to make the country see that he could favor the French fight for liberty without condoning the excesses that went with it. When all is

said, however, probably his chief failures as a political manager can be traced to three factors. He had a hasty, impulsive nature, which prevented his asking himself in every
juncture what was the discreet thing to do. He failed to con-
centrate upon political problems. He had a passion for the
rights of humanity.

This latter factor led him to espouse the cause of political
liberty in a age of reaction. It also led him to take inter-
nationalistic views, when such breadth of vision was unheard
of. His open rejoicings over American victories during the
ministry of North could be excused somewhat on the grounds
that the colonists, too, were Englishmen. But, there were
very few Englishmen who did not regard him as an open
enemy to his country when he expressed equal joy in the victories of the French over England and her allies. On this
subject, Coleridge wrote an open letter to him on November
4, 1802, in which he said: "Your defences, your palliations,
your phraseology, would have been plainly impolitic and of-
fensive had they been just and precise; and being too often
incorrect or overstrained they were injuries to yourself, and
to the glorious cause which you were pleading, to the cause
of peace, of freedom and of the independence of nations in
their domestic concerns." Fox himself wrote to his nephew
in the following month in terms which show how futile his
tactics were: "I mentioned in my last how I was threatened
in case I spoke warmly for peace, and if those threats were
not realized, it was not for want of inclination in the war-
riors. 'Apologist of France,' 'agent of the First Consul,' 'no
dislike of the power of France,' were dealt about pretty well
both in newspapers and in the House. . . . " Probably, Fox
did not realize how narrowly insular the English people
were in his time; or perhaps he did know, and deliberately

placed principle above success. At any rate, he would undoubtedly have had more popularity at home if he had had less of it among the Jacobins in France, or in the Court of Catherine the Great of Russia. The age was not yet ripe for a statesman of cosmopolitan views.

A fifth handicap for Fox was his natural violence in debate, which led him to overstate his opinions and gave the effect of personal acrimony to what was in reality only uncontrolled sincerity. Moritz, when he visited Parliament, was much shocked by the invectives he heard. Fox's admiring biographer, Lord John Russell, reluctantly admitted that the policy of using invectives "was very questionable," as "they in some measure created a diversion in favour" of George III and his ministers. Fox himself felt that violence was useless or even harmful in debate, but insisted that it could not be avoided. "We live in times of violence and of extremes," he wrote to his nephew, in 1793, "and all those who are for creating or even retaining checks upon power are considered as enemies to order. However, one must do one's duty, and one must endeavour to do it without passion, but everything in Europe appears to my ideas so monstrous that it is difficult to think of things calmly even alone, much more to discuss them so, when heated by dispute. Good God! that a man should be sent to Botany Bay for advising another to read Paine's book, or for reading the Irish address at a public meeting!" Thus the goodness of his heart, the strength of his convictions, resulted in a violence of temper which contrasted unfavorably with the customary judicial calm of Pitt.

Finally may be cited the character of Fox's genius, which fitted him naturally for attack rather than for defense; for piercing through the weaknesses and absurdities of the plans of another, rather than for the careful construction of plans

of his own. This, at least, is the conception of his character
held by many of his contemporaries. It is contradicted in part
by Fox's care and industry during the brief periods he held
office. It is supported, however, by his many tactical blunders
as minority leader, by the impulsiveness of his nature, and by
his innate preference for private life rather than public responsibilities.

In sum, then, it may be concluded that Fox, for all his
great natural gifts, did not use them to the best political advantage. Perhaps he counted his loss of the highest success
not too great a price to pay for the pleasures of his youth, and
the domestic happiness of his later life. His public achievements were very great; his public failures were counter-bal-
anced by private gains. He has come down through history as
the man who established and gave direction to the great
English Liberal party, and he died content. Disappointed as
he was over many issues, he probably would not have hesi-
tated over the question of whether his was a satisfying life.

Chapter 9 — Player Off Stage

The question of whether Sheridan actually was a persuasive speaker is perhaps the hardest puzzle the oratory of that period offers. There are two strong traditions respecting it. On the one hand is the tradition that Sheridan did no more than amuse the House, that he was, as De Quincey said, "a mocking bird through the entire scale." This was exactly the point of view of George Gilfillan, who wrote so soon after Sheridan's death as to be acquainted with the contemporary estimate of him. Gilfillan declared roundly that "Sheridan's whole existence was a farce. . . . He was a mountebank of amazing talent," an "adventurer who exhibited on the parliamentary stage." Mrs. Oliphant concluded that Sheridan was "a light-hearted adventurer in politics as well as in life, with keen perceptions and a brilliant way of now and then hitting out a right suggestion, and finding often a fine and effective thing to say. It is impossible, however, to think of him as influencing public opinion in any great or lasting way." Lord Brougham agreed with this view. He wrote of Sheridan: "as a statesman, he is without a place in any class, or of any rank; it would be incorrect and flattering to call him a bad, or hurtful, or a short-sighted, or a middling statesman; he was no statesman at all." It appears to be undisputed that Parliament sometimes refused to take him seriously. On one occasion, the members laughed outright when he and Dundas, neither of whom knew more than a smattering of French, undertook to dispute the meaning of the word "malheureux." The fact of his "comparative lack of weight and influence" is attested by the lack of any great successful measures associated with his name. It is also true that Sheridan failed to establish his political importance in the eyes of his literary critics, who dismiss his last thirty-two years with a sigh of regret that he abandoned literature for so unprofitable a field of endeavor.

Yet there is another tradition which, if not equally strong, is perhaps better supported by facts. This is noted in the journal of Wraxall, who said that "Sheridan won his way by a sort of fascination." An anecdote has been preserved by Walter Sickel to illustrate Sheridan's effectiveness with his constituents, in his first election campaign, and afterwards:

"Sheridan's raillery, it was said, converted hostile strangers in stagecoaches. He humoured the crowd, and laughed prejudices out of court. But a much later incident of the hustings — probably when Paull, the tailor's son, opposed him at Westminster — has never been recorded, and may illustrate his good humour now (1780), though it happened long afterwards. 'I should like to dash that fellow's brains out,' coarsely exclaimed the vituperator. Sheridan waited his turn and then quietly observed: 'You have heard the candidate's amiable desire. I cordially agree, and have only one request to submit. Let him be very careful when he performs his operation. Let him pick up my brains, for he needs them sadly.' "

Sheridan's son, Tom, bore striking testimony to his powers when he said, "No man can listen to my father and retain a judgment of his own." Lord Byron was much struck by his persuasive ability, and declared, "There has been nothing like it since the days of Orpheus; he could soften the heart of an attorney." Sheridan's biographers list a great number of instances in which he employed his persuasiveness with practical effectiveness upon his creditors. On the death of his friend Richardson, when Sheridan arrived too late for the funeral, "the agony of his grief" actually prevailed on the curate to reread the service.

That this magic power was carried over into Parliament is amply attested. In 1805, when Sheridan denounced Pitt for his treachery in abandoning the Catholics, Pitt's eyes "started from their sockets and seemed to tell him if he advanced an atom further he would have his life." On the occasion of the first Begum speech, on February 7, 1787, he achieved the greatest oratorical triumph on record. As Sichel describes the scene, "Over five hundred members were present when, at midnight, Sheridan rose. A stillness succeeded in which a pin could be heard to drop. For nearly six hours he riveted his audience by an utterance exceedingly rapid though singularly distinct, and at the close his voice sank to a whisper. The House, for the first time within record, broke into applause, and Sheridan's friends rushed up to him and hung about his neck." Two days later, Horace Walpole wrote to Lady Ossory, Sheridan "talked for five hours and a half on Wednesday, and turned everybody's head. One heard everybody in the streets raving on the wonders of that speech." So moved were the members that they dared not vote until their wits were restored, and moved a recess until the following day. Fox objected to the absurdity of postponing a vote "for no other reason than had been alleged, than because members were too firmly convinced,"but Pitt insisted on adjournment.

More astonishing than this success was the fact that a year

later he could deliver the same charge in the course of the
Hastings trial, before the Lords, without either repeating
himself, or striking an anti-climax. So great was his fame
now that lords and ladies were up by six A.M., paid fifty
guineas for tickets, and were in their seats in the galleries by
eleven o'clock, although he was scheduled to speak at two.
This speech was divided into four parts, and delivered on
June 3, 6, 10, and 13, 1788. Its effectiveness was described
by Sheridan's wife, in a letter to his sister: "It is impossible,
my dear woman, to convey to you the delight, the astonishment, the adoration, he has excited in the breasts of every
class of people. Even party prejudice has been overcome by
a display of genius, eloquence and goodness which no one
with anything like a heart about them could have listened to
without being the wiser and the better for the rest of their
lives. . . . " Wraxall, writing of this speech, said "The most
ardent admirers of Burke, of Fox and of Pitt allowed that
they had been outdone as orators by Sheridan." Sir Gilbert
Elliot declared, "I am now convinced that his powers in this
kind are far beyond any other man's, and that nobody living
could execute what he did yesterday." An anonymous contemporary says that after this speech "his superiority over his
colleagues was established by universal consent." Had the
Lords voted upon Hastings at that time, they would probably have convicted him. But the trial dragged on for six
more years, at which time no particular speech could have
had much effect on the verdict.

Although it was Sheridan's misfortune to spend practically his whole political life in hopeless opposition to the sway
of Pitt, he can scarcely be adjudged unpersuasive for that
reason. His biographer Thomas Moore stated the case as

favorably, but also as fairly, as it well could be stated, shortly after Sheridan's death:

"If to watch over the rights of the subject, and guard them against the encroachments of power, be, even in safe and ordinary times, a task full of usefulness and honour, how much more glorious to have stood sentinel over the same sacred trust, through a period so trying as that with which Sheridan had to struggle — when liberty itself had become suspected and unpopular — when authority had succeeded in identifying patriotism with treason, and when the few remaining and deserted friends of freedom were reduced to take their stand on a narrowing isthmus, between anarchy on one side and the angry incursions of power on the other. How manfully he maintained his ground in a position so critical, the annals of England and of the champions of her constitution will long testify. The truly national spirit, too, with which, when that struggle was past, and the dangers to liberty from without seemed greater than any from within, he forgot all past differences, in the one common cause of Englishmen, and while others 'gave but the left hand to the country,' proffered her both of his, stamped a seal of sincerity on his public conduct, which, in the eyes of all England, authenticated it as genuine patriotism."

In summing up his conclusions as to Sheridan's persuasiveness, Sadler said of him that "Neglected as a politician, slandered as a man, Sheridan nevertheless received as a speaker full, perhaps excessive recognition. In an age of oratory and among a society of orators, his supremacy was almost universally acknowledged." It is doubtful whether we are justified in separating Sheridan the politician from Sheridan the orator, as Sadler did. To the extent that his speaking failed in political effectiveness, it failed in persuasive power.

Probably no matter how persuasive he might have been, he could not have swept Pitt from his secure hold on the ministry. It is significant that no more than Burke was he considered worthy of a seat in the cabinet, during the two brief periods of his career that his friends were in power. The explanation for this relative ineffectiveness is found chiefly in four personal factors.

His reputation was throughout his parliamentary career a political handicap. It was attacked upon three bases. First, there was the fact that he entered Parliament as a brilliant and successful playwright and theatre manager. The other members rather resented his intrusion. Their sense of dignity was outraged. Even his friend, Samuel Woodfall, the printer, told him after his first long speech, "I am sorry to say I do not think that this is your line—you had much better have stuck to your former pursuits." This feeling was doubtless accentuated by the fact that Sheridan's father, also, was an actor, and a teacher of elocution. His connections had all been with a speech of display, rather than of deliberation and purpose. It occasioned no surprise to the House when, in debate on a plan to tax the incomes of pensioners and placemen, on April 8, 1794, a Mr. Rose sneeringly referred to Sheridan as "manager of his theatre, or . . . as a man who travelled the country with his puppet-show at his back." Sheridan protested against the allusion, but must have felt helpless in the face of the deep-seated prejudice which it revealed.

His reputation also suffered from the instability of his character, his gambling, his drinking, and his chronic indebtedness. True, he was no worse in any of these respects than many of his colleagues; but for some reason they were condemned rather more in him than in the others. His indebtedness, for instance, was not as great as that of Fox, Burke, or Pitt, yet stories of how he was hounded by constables and creditors abound, and he was always considered especially culpable. Probably one reason for this was his strong tendency to joke about his financial troubles, and to make them the butt of his humor. On one occasion, for instance, he wrote an "I. O. U." for a creditor with the remark, "There, that's settled." Again, when a creditor rode up to him on a fine horse and demanded his money, Sheridan diverted the subject by remarking that he might like to buy the horse for his wife, and suggested that the man show off her paces. As soon as the creditor had ridden off a little distance for this purpose, Sheridan slipped away. He is reported to have replied to a creditor who peremptorily demanded payment of the interest on a long-standing loan, "My dear Sir, you know it is not my interest to pay the principal; nor is it my principle to pay the interest." So freely was his character discussed and censured that it was made the subject of comment in court, by one of the greatest lawyers of the day. Sheridan was being sued by his co-proprieters of Drury Lane Theatre in 1799, and defended his case in person. As Sanders tells the story, Sheridan "won an oratorical triumph in a totally untried field. But he had to submit to comments on his improvidence from the defendant's counsel, Mr. Mansfield, which wounded him to the quick; while the Lord Chancellor, in tones of fatherly admonition, applied to him the concluding words of Johnson's 'Life of Savage': 'Negligence and irregularity long-continued will make knowledge useless, wit ridiculous, and genius contemptible.' " The third harmful element in Sheridan's reputation was the continued suspicion of his audience that he was insincere, and merely speaking to display his wit and cleverness. This arose in part from his former profession, in part from the apparent examples of just this attitude in his speeches. In the sense in which De Quincey considered the distinction, Sheridan was believed to be rhetorical, rather than eloquent. Mrs. Oliphant wrote rather naively in 1902 that "Nobody, so far as we are aware, has ever doubted Sheridan's honesty or the sincerity of his political convictions." Other biographers, however, found that insincerity was one of the chief charges made against Sheridan by his contemporaries. "Men were suspicious of his easy address and invariable geniality," wrote Michael Sadler, "regarding them as proofs of insincerity." De Quincey, as we have seen, was certain that Sheridan was insincere. So was Gilfillan. J. W. Fortesque could see little sincerity in any of the prosecutors of Hastings. We are told in regard to Sheridan's effect on his parliamentary audience that "The hardheaded Tories asked for facts, and on receiving instead wit and eloquence, smiled, shrugged, and turned away." Pitt did not hesitate to characterize Sheridan openly in Parliament as one "in most of whose speeches there was much fancy, in many shining wit, in others very ingenious argument, in all great eloquence, and in some few truths and justice." Hence it would appear that Sheridan was characterized by his colleagues as a dramatic wit, as an impecunious drunkard, and as an insincere rhetorician, all of which charges militated against his persuasive effectiveness.

Besides these personal liabilities, he was ultimately discredited, and almost ruined, by his adherence to the Prince of Wales. The Prince was a dissolute wastrel who lived in perpetual enmity with his father the King. He joined himself to the party of the Foxite Whigs, in order to have their influence in Parliament, and they eagerly strengthened the connection, in the expectation that he would favor them when he came to the throne. Sheridan in particular was the close counsellor and companion of the Prince. But the Prince's character was so dissipated and immoral, his extravagances so costly to the nation, his relations with his father so unfilial that all his associates were discredited in Parliament and before the country. This was strikingly illustrated in Sheridan's experience during the Regency fight in 1788. Sheridan's zeal moved him to warn the House against temporizing, lest the

Prince be moved to "assert his right." Pitt immediately arose and characterized this remark as "an indecent menace thrown out to awe and influence the proceedings of the House." Grenville wrote of Sheridan's hapless speech to this effect: "It was such a blunder that I never knew any man of the meanest talents guilty of before. During the whole time that I have sat in Parliament I have never seen such an uproar as was raised by his threatening." In effect, the Prince used Sheridan as his cat's paw, and abandoned him to misery in the years following Fox's death.

Sheridan's lack of a strong feeling of partisanship was both a help and a hindrance to his parliamentary effectiveness. During his first years in Parliament, he was a firm and unvarying Whig. But after his brilliant success in his speech indicting Hastings, in 1787, he felt an increasing degree of indifference to the ties of party. His opinion of Fox as the party leader is clearly expressed in his speech on the Army Estimates, of December 8, 1802. "I perfectly agree with my honorable friend that war ought to be avoided, though he does not agree with me on the means best calculated to produce that effect. From any opinion he may express, I never differ but with the greatest reluctance. For him my affection, my esteem, and my attachment, are unbounded, and they will end only with my life." Nevertheless he did differ with him, on this occasion and many other times. How Sheridan suffered in the opinions of his colleagues by such deviations from partisan loyalty is revealed in a letter which Fox wrote to his nephew concerning this speech. "Sheridan made a very foolish speech," he wrote, "if a speech full of wit can be with propriety so called, upon the Army Estimates, of which all who wish him ill are as fond as I, who wish him well, am vexed at it. He will, however, I do not doubt, be still right in the end." Others, of course, were inclined to trust and respect him all the more, for placing his convictions above his party.

As clear evidence that there was nothing in any respect dishonorable in Sheridan's laxity of political affiliation, we have the fact that he deliberately chose poverty with the Whigs to affluence and office with the Tories. At any time, he would have been welcomed into the Tory group, as were the "Old Whigs" in 1792. However, Sheridan stated his own situation, amid tears, in the hearing of Lord Byron, during his last year. "Sir, it is easy for my Lord G(renville) or Earl G(rey), or Marquis B. (of Bath), or Lord H(ertford), with thousands a year—some of it presently derived or *inherited* in sinecures or acquisitions from the public money, to boast of their patriotism and keep aloof from temptation; but they do not know from what temptations those have kept aloof who had equal pride, at least equal talents and not unequal passions, and nevertheless knew not in the course of their lives what it was to have a shilling of their own." But disinterested, sincere, and patriotic as his independence was, it resulted in Fox's losing confidence in him, and the Tories never came to trust him. So, his effectiveness was weakened.

Finally, Sheridan was handicapped by his sincere and passionate defence of human rights. In his denunciation of the royal prerogative, his sympathy with the poor, his belief in taxation of the rich, and his hatred of injustice in any form, Sheridan was definitely ahead of his age. When he organized the Society of the Friends of the People to spread the doctrines of Jacobinism in England, he only hurt the Whig cause and lessened his own chances of political advancement. He asserted in one of his speeches that "the poorest people in the kingdom, were those who stood most in need of friends in that house." This was so true that in espousing their cause Sheridan found himself advancing beyond the reach of his party's support. In this respect he was like Burke, in that his greatest actual contribution to his country was a handicap to his political success.

In the satirical poems, lampoons and cartoons of that time, Sheridan's love of drink, poverty, debts, republicanism, insincerity, and theatricality were chiefly emphasized.

Sheridan's persuasiveness, then, no more than Burke's or Fox's depended chiefly upon the rhetorical qualities in his speeches. Behind the speeches themselves stood the man, with his foibles, his personality, and his reputation. Sometimes these factors united with the brilliancy of his speech to produce an overwhelming success. More often, they militated against a success he could otherwise have won.

Chapter 10—Genius in Ice

Judged in terms of obvious achievement Pitt had an extraordinarily successful career. He was a cabinet member at twenty-three, prime minister at twenty-five, chief of state for nineteen of the twenty-five years he spent in Parliament and, on the whole, a uniquely efficient party leader. What greater success could a man want? A glance below the surface indicates that Pitt wanted a great deal that he did not get. He was far from being what one enthusiastic biographer entitled him, "England's Greatest Statesman." There was a strange mixture of the effective and the ineffective in his character.

Insofar as he wanted position, recognition, and ostensible power, he did achieve his goal. Insofar as he desired the real power to carry out his ideals, he dismally failed. One of his ideals was to balance the budget and make England economically secure. This he might well have accomplished had he not been forced by circumstances into the ruinous French war. That upset his Sinking Fund plan and piled up both debts and taxes. Pitt might have been a very great minister of peace; he was less suited for the role he had to play as a minister of war.

His real failure, however, lay far deeper than the accident of his being a contemporary of Napoleon. It consisted of the completeness and apparent ease of his sacrifice of his Whig principles. Although his father led the revolt against the Walpole Whig oligarchy, he had created a tradition of new Whig independence, and in that tradition Pitt had grown up. Naturally, Pitt entered Parliament in 1781 as a Whig, in opposition to Lord North and the American War. When Rockingham's death split the Whigs into the Foxites and the Chathamites under Lord Shelburne, Pitt just as naturally followed Shelburne. But Shelburne held office only by sufferance of the strongly Tory King, and in the subsequent battles between the Fox-North coalition and the Shelburne ministry Pitt found himself inevitably grouped with the reactionaries. Only the liberal Tories could follow North into his allegiance with Fox, just as the conservative Whigs were forced away from Fox into the Opposition. Hence, at the dissolution of the Coalition, when Pitt succeeded to the post of prime minister, he was supported first of all by all the pensioners and placemen who were creatures of the crown, and secondly by the reactionary members of both parties. Pitt could not have relished the situation, yet he either desired office so much or considered his own incumbency so essential to the country that he accepted it.

Pitt's position as prime minister was but little stronger than that of Lord North during the American War. Both held office only so long as George III pleased to keep them there. Within certain limits Pitt could rule the country as he pleased. But those limits were rigid, impassable, and they proved to exclude almost everything Pitt really wished to accomplish. He could not, for instance, carry out the parliamentary reform which his father had declared essential, and to which he had early pledged himself. He even was forced to curtail the liberties of the people far more than they had been since the days of the Stuarts. He could not accomplish the abolition of the slave trade, upon which he had set his heart. He was forced by the king shamefully to break an explicit bargain he had made with the Irish Catholics to grant them emancipation if they would vote for his plan of Irish Union. In securing the passage of the Union Bill in the Irish Parliament, he (who was personally incorruptible) had to employ bribery as freely as had the very Walpole his father had spent years in condemning. He had to abandon his economic principles to finance a long and ineffective war in Europe. In short, Pitt had to give up his liberalism and become founder of the modern Tory party—the spiritual forebear of Castlereagh, Canning, Wellington, Peel and Disraeli.

The historian Robertson sums up other aspects of his failure in sentimental terms: "The tears of human beings, of pathos and tragedy, haunt the career of this solitary man, dwelling apart on the heights of great affairs; who never knew the love of wife or child; who worked so hard in the golden promise of his political apprenticeship for peace, retrenchment, and reform; who in the maturity of his powers constituted himself the champion of a cause that linked continuous war abroad with repression and reaction at home, with swollen debt and bloated armaments; who died in the bitter knowledge that popular liberties had been suspended, the National Debt more than doubled, taxation strained to the breaking point, a quarter of a million of human lives sacrificed, and that peace and reform were further out of sight than ever; bitterest of all, that the old order in Europe had perished and that Napoleon, the incarnate spirit of the French Revolution, was triumphant over two-thirds of the Continent."

It is difficult to maintain a nice balance in the judgment of Pitt. He failed in so much and he succeeded in so much that by overlooking one side or the other critics easily obtain a false view. The perspective needs to include both sides. The following summary of the handicaps that kept Pitt from achieving complete success will provide a necessary basis for future consideration of his rhetorical methods of persuasion.

Pitt's arrogance, haughtiness, pride, coldness, and air of strict reserve exercised even toward his political colleagues prevented him from cementing with the bonds of affection a closely-knit following. These qualities he inherited in full measure from his father, who, in his later years aroused such intense feelings of dislike that he could hardly find friends enough to compose his last cabinet. Like Woodrow Wilson, whose character and career interestingly parallels his in many respects, Pitt was very friendly and congenial among intimates, but presented only a frozen exterior to most of his associates. This probably was an attempt to maintain his dignity and prestige among men of higher rank and wider political experience than himself; it may also have resulted in part from his solitary, unsocial childhood. That it was often a serious handicap in his political career cannot be denied.

Pitt's youth when he came to power was a subject of amazement to his contemporaries, and formed an impression against which he was forced to combat constantly. Thus on December 5, 1782, after he had been made Chancellor of the Exchequer in Shelburne's cabinet, he opened his first speech in office by saying, "There were several things un-

fortunate in his situation on that day, but the calamity
under which he chiefly laboured was his youth; a calamity
he could not sufficiently lament, as it had been made the subject of animadversion on the other side of the house. His
youth, he allowed, was very exceptionable to that situation;
yet he trusted the system of his conduct, and his strict dis-
charge of the duties of his high office, would in a great measure do away with what he felt himself to be an objection,
but which at the same time he pledged himself would be as
far as possible provided for, by his care, industry, and assidu-
ity, and a faithful observance of the real good and interests
of his country, which should ever hold the first place in his
contemplation." It will not be forgotten that his father,
when ten years older than Pitt was at this age, had to defend
himself against Horatio Walpole on a similar charge, in the
speech commencing, "My Lords, I have been accused of the
atrocious crime of being a young man." Such, too, was the
"atrocious crime" attributed to the Younger Pitt.

Pitt was often charged with failure to understand human
nature, and this reputed lack of sympathy proved a subject
of attack upon him. Speaking hypothetically, on a motion to
repeal the bill suspending the Habeas Corpus Act, on January 5, 1795, Sheridan gave a veiled description of Pitt. "I can
suppose the case of a haughty and stiff-necked minister," he
said, "who never mixed in a popular assembly, who had
therefore no common feeling with the mass of the people,
no knowledge of the mode in which their intercourse was
conducted, who was not a month in the ranks in this house
before he was raised to the first situation, and though on a
footing of equality with every other member, elevated with
the idea of fancied superiority; such a minister can have no
communication with the people of England, except through

the medium of spies and informers; he is unacquainted with
the mode in which their sentiments are expressed, and cannot make allowance for the language of toasts and resolutions adopted in an unguarded and convivial hour. Such a
minister, if he lose their confidence, he will bribe their hate;
if he disgust them by arbitrary measures, he will not leave
them till they are completely bound and shackled; above all,
he will gratify the vindictive resentment of apostacy, by
prosecuting all those who dare to espouse the cause which he
has betrayed, and he will not desist from the gratification of
his malignant propensities, and the prosecution of his arbitrary schemes, till he has buried in one grave the peace, the
happiness, the glory, and the independence of England.
Such a minister must be disqualified to judge of the real state
of the country, and must be eternally the dupe of those vile
spies, whose interest it is to deceive him as well as to betray
others." The astute Miss Berry similarly noted in her journal that "Perhaps his greatest errors originated from his
early and constant immersion in public business, and from
his having been always an actor, never a spectator of affairs."

It is probably true, too, that Pitt's intellect was of a character which does not impel its possessor on to the leadership
of new causes. Perhaps because of the immense pressure exerted upon him by the weight of official responsibility and
continual labor, he was content to be a follower fully as
much as a leader. At any rate, he was in no single instance
the originator of a new crusade. Robertson, in summarizing
Pitt's career, pointed out: "In finance and economic reform
he applied the ideas of Adam Smith, Burke, Shelburne,
Price; Chatham, Saville, Wilkes, Richmond, Fox taught the
nation the programme of electoral reform; the splendid
failure of Fox and Burke was the basis of his India Bill; to

the making of his Irish policy contributed many workers—
Grattan, Cornwallis, Castlereagh; he learned the abomina-
tions of the slave trade from Wilberforce and Clarkson; his
later foreign policy was profoundly influenced by Grenville;
as a 'War Minister' he was dominated, to England's cost, by
Dundas. And this assimilative quality had its conspicuous
disadvantages. . . . Only once, in 1800, in his career did he
sacrifice office for a principle; and it is significant that the
abolition of the slave trade was advocated but not effected by
the Minister who was in power for seventeen years, but carried by his rival who was in power for half as many months."
However much an administrator may gain from able and
willing helpers in formulating his policies, there is a strength
gained only by the crusading enthusiasm born of strong in-
ner convictions. This strength Pitt seemed to lack.

Finally, in assessing the failures of Pitt, prime consideration must be given to the instability of his political following. Very few of them were bound to him by any kind of
personal ties. Most of them fell into one of two groups:
either self-seeking adventurers who supported the government—any government—for the advantages they could
gain, or adherents of the King who required of Pitt a fun-
damental subservience to the arbitrary will and considerably
detailed political opinions of George III. In contrast to this
uneasy and unstable coalition of Pittites was the devotion
which bound Fox's followers to him by strong personal ties.
Thus Fox was able to tack and veer in his opposition policies,
whereas Pitt must always consider whether he might be out-
stepping the bounds of the path his party would permit him
to tread.

These factors include the main explanations for Pitt's failure to attain greater stature as a political leader. But he did

achieve a remarkable success in the length and tenacity of his tenure of office. He must have had uncommon powers and advantages to balance the defects and handicaps that have been cited. He was, in fact, aided by tremendous personal advantages, as well as by a fortunate combination of accidental and external factors, some of which may be singled out and identified.

First of all, he was greatly helped by the influence of his father's fame. Lord Chatham remained a symbol to conjure with in English politics long after he was dead. Much was expected of his son; much, undoubtedly was assumed regarding the son of such a father. To have fallen below the family tradition would have been a grievous fault, but the tradition itself aided in buoying him up—just as the tradition of the Adams family in America has aided the successive inheritors of its name.

Next in consideration is Pitt's own character, which, it has been pointed out, was partly a handicap to him. But it was also partly a help. His disdain for money may have permitted his servants to cheat him outrageously, and resulted in the piling up of a huge debt for his country later to pay. It also saved him from any imputation of personal corruptibility, and made possible the dramatic gesture with which he commenced his career, of refusing to profit at the public expense. Similarly, his cool, dignified, proud and commanding manner gave him early the prestige needed to control older men. Like his father, he was made to command, and he managed to convince his associates of that fact while he was still little more than a youth.

One element of his character which deserves separate consideration was his consuming ambition. This formed the great drive of his career. As a mere boy, when his father was

elevated to the peerage, he exclaimed that he was glad he
was not the oldest son, for he wished to speak in the House
of Commons as his father had done. This ambition overcame
the effects of ill-health, propelled him through a tremendous course of study, and stimulated his mastery of argument and the forms of public speech. It led to his rejection
of the felicities of marriage, and centered all his energies in
the single channel of his political career. This element of his
character was in striking contrast to the easy-going, pleasure-
loving Fox. Horace Walpole, who knew them both well,
drew a comparison of them in July, 1782, which stresses
this point:

"Young as Fox was, Pitt was ten years younger; and what a fund of
knowledge and experience were ten years in possession of such a master
genius as Fox, besides the prodigious superiority of solid parts! Yet Fox
left by neglect some advantages to Pitt. The one trusted to his natural
abilities, and, whenever he wanted, never found them to fail; Pitt, on
the contrary, attended to nothing but the means of gratifying his ambition. . . . Fox seemed to leave pleasure with regret, and to bestow
only spare moments on the government of a nation; Pitt to make industry and virtue the ladders of his ambition. Fox's greatness was innate; and if he had ambition, it was the only passion which he took no
pains to gratify. . . . Pitt cultivated friends to form a party."

Pitt's great ability to either clarify or obscure the issue under discussion was one of his best political assets. As to the
first, simple clarity is often the most effective device for persuasion.* As for the second, once the trust of his followers

*Thus, Edgar Allen Poe, in his "A Chapter of Suggestions," *Works*
VII, pp. 331-332, New York, 1927, wrote: "A precise or *clear man*, in
conversation or in composition, has a very important consequential advantage—more especially in matters of logic. As he proceeds with his
argument, the person addressed, exactly comprehending, for that reason,
and often for that reason only, agrees. Few minds, in fact, can immediately perceive the distinction between the comprehension of a proposition and an agreement of the reason with the thing proposed. Pleased
at comprehending, we often are so excited as to take it for granted that
we assent."

had been won, it was a great advantage to be able to involve them neatly in a web of words, on points which would not bear clear examination.

One of the chief external factors in Pitt's success was the fact that he occupied a point of mediation between George the Third and Fox. George seized upon him in 1783 as the one barrier by which he could keep Fox from office. This continued to be the chief reason for George's favor toward Pitt during all the years until Fox's temporary loss of power in 1792. Then Pitt seemed the only man strong enough to control the state during the fever of Jacobinism accompanying the first years of the French Revolution. When this fever had died down, and George felt that the government could safely be trusted to other hands, he did not hesitate to drive Pitt from power on the issue of toleration for the Irish Catholics. It is doubtless true that had the Opposition been either less powerful or less personally obnoxious to George, Pitt would not have found his attainment of the premiership so easy, or his hold upon it so secure.

Pitt exhibited remarkable political astuteness in capitalizing upon these advantages. In the fight with the Foxites in the early part of 1784, he unquestionably jockeyed them from a strongly entrenched position. With the aid of the East India Company's propaganda, he destroyed the public's confidence in them. Also, in the Regency battle of 1788, when he came near to losing his place, he managed through a remarkable combination of political astuteness and luck to delay the appointment of the Prince of Wales as Regent, and again to destroy confidence in the Whigs. Before his subterfuges were exhausted, the King recovered, and that danger was past. In the decisive struggle of 1783-1784, Fox made one mistake after another, while Pitt displayed skill, patience, courage and parliamentary ability such as few other British statesmen have ever shown.

Pitt's willingness to accept the "second best"—in sharp contrast to the high-souled, if politically unwise, idealism of Burke—was also a considerable factor in his success. This willingness to compromise, to give up his Whig principles when they interfered with his control of the House, to accept the main lines of the Tory program, contributed to set the cause of reform in England back fifty years. This attitude deprived Pitt of his truest claim to greatness and his country's gratitude. But, nonetheless, it was a chief factor in securing the prime ministry for him.

Finally, one more of Pitt's weaknesses may be found parodoxically as a source of his political strength. If he failed to understand the English character in many respects, he at least was superior to Fox, Sheridan, and Burke in sensing the narrow insularity of the British viewpoint. Whereas, Burke spent his genius in trying to interest the English in the wrongs of peoples across the seas, and whereas, Fox and Sheridan took an international viewpoint in the French wars, Pitt was first and foremost nationalistic. Pitt only once set foot off of English soil, and then only for a period of six weeks. Hence, he had little opportunity to develop a cosmopolitan attitude. While the Foxites were arguing about justice for mankind during the French war, Pitt kept firmly in mind the three cardinal, intensely English principles upon which alone he would accede to peace. These were: establishment of a balance of power in Europe; restoration of the *status quo* in Europe; and unrestricted opportunity for British expansion outside of Europe. With this point of view, he made a direct appeal to the Tory squires who formed the bulk of Parliament, especially when the Foxites made the mistake of openly rejoicing over the victories won by the French.

In concluding this preliminary survey of persuasive factors in the character and situation of Pitt, there is one more significant fact to be noted. His failure to carry through Parliament the measures of his own choice demonstrates clearly that he was no more successful than were Burke, Fox and Sheridan in "winning" votes against the corruptly entrenched power of the King. The Tory majority was too heavily set to be moved by anything short of the almost revolutionary storm of public opinion such as finally carried the reform bills of the 1830's. Pitt's success looms so large because he merely had to hold these votes in line; to supply the rationalizations by which this majority justified its votes to itself and, rarely, to its constituents. It cannot be denied that this task was far from being a contemptible one, in the face of one of the most determined and able Oppositions which any era has produced, nor that Pitt accomplished it brilliantly. It is in terms of this task that his persuasive effectiveness must finally be measured.

Part Four

Their Methods

Chapter 11—The Artist

Burke had two principal, and opposite, methods of per-
suation which he used, respectively, as the occasion or the
warmth of his temper warranted. One was to employ the
overpowering force of relentless logic, bolstered by biting
invective, sarcasm, irony, and marshalled arrays of facts.
This was his method in his speeches on American Taxation,
on Fox's East India Bill, and on the Nabob of Arcot's Debts.
His other method was a conciliatory approach to the immediate problem, through emphasis upon a common goal, accompanied by every possible concession, every excuse for his
opponent's mistakes, assumption of as many common agree-
ments as possible, and withal the gentle but persistent pressure of the facts, supported by an analysis of the expediency
of his proposal. This method he employed in his speeches

on Conciliation with the Colonies, on Economical Reform, and to his constituents at Bristol in 1774 and 1780.

His two major speeches on America form a striking contrast and illustrate very well the two methods he used. The first was occasioned on April 19, 1774, by Mr. Roe Fuller's motion to tax all tea sold in the American colonies, the action that led to the Boston Tea Party. Burke arose in the midst of a warm debate, immediately following Charles Wolfram Cornwall, one of the lords of the treasury, and addressed his remarks directly to him. His introduction was a scathing denunciation of Cornwall's "disgusting argument," and proceeded thence to a pitiless, sarcastic, and contemptuous review of the long train of contradictory, pusillanimous, and undiplomatic stages in England's taxation policy toward the colonies during the previous decade.

The quotation of one brief paragraph will give a fair clue to the tone of the whole speech.

"Sir," said Burke, "it is not a pleasant consideration; but nothing in the world can read so awful and so instructive a lesson, as the conduct of ministry in this business, upon the mischief of not having large and liberal ideas in the management of great affairs. Never have the servants of the state looked at the whole of your complicated interests in one connected view. They have taken things by bits and scraps, some at one time and one pretence, and some at another, just as they pressed, without any sort of regard to their relation or dependencies. They never had any kind of system, right or wrong; but only invented occasionally some miserable tale for the day, in order meanly to sneak out of difficulties, into which they had proudly strutted. And they were put to all of these shifts and devices, full of meanness and full of mischief, in order to pilfer piecemeal a repeal of an act, which they had not the generous courage, when they found and felt their error, honourably and fairly to disclaim. By such management, by the irresistible operation of feeble councils, so paltry a sum as three-pence in the eyes of a financier, so insignificant an article as tea in the eyes of a philosopher, have shaken the pillars of a commercial empire that circled the whole globe."

Nor did Burke hesitate to contrast the base actions of the Tories with virtues of the brief-lived first Rockingham Ministry, which had repealed the stamp act. Describing that day, Burke declared, "I never came with so much spirits into this House. It was a time for a *man* to act in. We had powerful enemies; but we had faithful and determined friends; and a glorious cause. We had a great battle to fight; but we had the means of fighting; not as now, when our arms are tied behind us. We did fight that day and conquer." Such a speech still sparkles with life, and must have been exhiliarating to hear. When Burke offered to stop, there were cries of "Go on, go on." The speech was not the type to win votes.

Burke himself must have realized this, for his great appeal for Conciliation with the Colonies, on March 22, 1775, was as conciliatory as its title. His introduction was exalted in tone and wholly lacking in animosity. "We are therefore called upon, as it were by a superior warning voice, again to attend to America. . . . Surely it is an awful subject; or there is none so on this side of the grave. . . . My little share in this great deliberation oppressed me. I found myself a partaker in a very high trust." Upon this occasion he went on, "I persuaded myself that you would not reject a reasonable proposition because it had nothing but reason to recommend it. . . . I was very sure that, if my proposition were futile or dangerous, if it were weakly conceived, or improperly timed, there was nothing exterior to it, of power to awe, dazzle, or delude you. You will see it just as it is; and you will treat it just as it deserves. . . . The proposition is peace. . . . My idea is nothing more."

He then went on to show that "conciliation is admissible," for it had been sought by the ministry. Furthermore, the colonies were immensely valuable to England, as he showed by a review of their resources, their learning, and their spirit. It is true, they had been obstreperous, but there were only three possible means to meet that situation: change their spirit by removing its cause; prosecute it as criminal; or accept it as necessary. He went on to demonstrate that the first method was not feasible. As for the second, "I do not know the method," he confessed, "of drawing up an indictment against an whole people," therefore, "No way is open but the third and last—to comply with the American spirit as necessary." There is a natural reluctance to this course of action, but

"The question with me is, not whether you have a right to render your people miserable; but whether it is not your interest to make them happy. It is not what a lawyer tells me I *may* do; but what humanity, reason, and justice, tell me I ought to do. Is a politic act the worse for being a generous one? Is no concession proper, but that which is made from your want of right to keep what you grant?"

Finally he closed with an eloquent exordium, in which he divided his audience into two hypothetical groups, according to their attitude toward conciliation:

"All this, I know well enough, will sound wild and chimerical to the profane herd of those vulgar and mechanical politicians, who have not a place among us; a sort of people who think that nothing exists but what is gross and material; and who, therefore, far from being qualified to be directors of the great movement of empire, are not fit to turn a wheel in the machine. But to men truly initiated and rightly taught, these ruling and master principles, which, in the opinion of such men as I have mentioned, have no substantial existence, are in truth everything, and all in all. Magnanimity in politics is not seldom the truest wisdom; and a great empire and little minds go ill together. If we are conscious of our situation, and glow with zeal to fill our places as becomes our station and ourselves, we ought to auspicate all our public proceedings on America with the old warning of the Church, *Sursum Corda*! We ought to elevate our minds to the greatness of that trust to which the order of Providence has called us. By adverting to the dignity of this high calling, our ancestors have turned a savage wilderness into a glorious empire: and

have made the most extensive, and the only honourable conquests, not
by destroying, but by promoting the wealth, the number, the happiness
of the human race. Let us get an American revenue as we have got
an American empire. English privileges have made it all that it is;
English privileges alone will make it all that it can be."

As a matter of fact, this speech was no more successful
than the one on taxation in winning votes, and was less liked
by the audience. Its success has been won as literature, as an
historical document, as a masterpiece of political philosophy,
and as a great liberal thesis. Perhaps its chief disadvantge as
a speech was its inordinate length. Five hours was too long
for even Burke's friends to sit still. In the midst of the
speech, Sir Thomas Erskine slipped behind a row of seats
and slipped from the hall, unobserved by the fervid orator.
However, the 270 votes which were cast against Burke's motion, as compared to the 78 cast for it, were not a gauge of
the worth of the appeal, but of the corrupt impenetrability
of the ministerial party. Certainly from a psychological
point of view, Burke could hardly have been more conciliatory than he was in this speech, or more adroit in conceal-
ing criticism beneath generally accepted principles.

Burke's greatest speech, judged in terms of its immediate
accomplishments, was that which he delivered on February
11, 1780, in presenting his plan for Economical Reform. In
it he had two purposes: to reduce the heavy burden of taxation which had been largely increased during the American
war; and to reduce the corrupt influence of the crown. Both
these ends could be achieved by eliminating a great many
sinecure offices, reducing the number and size of pensions,
and consolidating state offices. In such a project, Burke was
certain to be opposed by all place-holders, by all who hoped
to obtain places, by the whole Tory party, and by all those
entrenched interests which favored the continuance of con-

trol by the crown. The task seemed hopeless. But Burke seized on a favorable moment to initiate his scheme, when the nation was tired of the war, was crying out against the terrible tax burden, and was showering petitions upon Parliament for reform. Furthermore, he took advantage of the tardy and reluctant responsiveness of Parliament to the popular will. This responsiveness was evidenced in the astonishing vote that carried Dunning's motion "that it is the opiinon of this committee that the influence of the crown has increased, is increasing, and ought to be diminished."

There were many demands for reform outside of Parliament demonstrating the spirit to which Burke addressed his appeal. In 1779-80, "Numerous county meetings" protested the high war taxes and called for economic reform. In December, 1779, both Richmond and Shelburne introduced bills demanding reform in the House of Lords. Both bills were overwhelmingly defeated. In December, 1779, 8,000 freeholders of York petitioned Parliament for reform. Very soon thereafter, twenty-three other counties, and eleven large towns took similar action. All factions of the Whigs united for this endeavor. Such manifestations gave Burke some hope of success, and he seriously undertook to persuade the place-men to vote for their own curtailment.

His introduction was about 1300 words long. It was devoted to demonstrating his own sincerity, disinterestedness, and lack of prospects for any political reward for his labors in this field. "I rise," he said, ". . . in conformity to the unanimous wishes of the whole nation . . . nothing in the world has led me to such an undertaking but my zeal for the honour of this House. . . . I advance to it with a tremor that shakes me to the inmost fibre of my frame. . . . I know that all parsimony is of a quality approaching to unkindness. . . ."

This is no pleasant prospect at the outset of a political jour-
ney . . . services of the present sort create no attachments . . .
the reformation will operate against the reformers. . . . Reformation is one of those pieces which must be put at some
distance in order to please. . . . I risk odium if I succeed, and
contempt if I fail."

Upon this conciliatory introduction, Burke immediately
built his first point. "My excuse must rest in my own and
your conviction of the absolute, urgent necessity there is,
that something of the kind should be done. . . . It is necessary from our own political circumstances; it is necessary
from the operations of the enemy; it is necessary from the
demands of the people. . . ." In developing these points,
Burke produced an example of perfect tact. Comparing English finances with French, to the great disparagement of the
former, he disclaimed "any invidious purpose. It is in order
to excite in us the spirit of a noble emulation. Let the nations make war upon each other (since we must make war),
not with a low and vulgar malignity, but by a competition of
virtues. This is the only way by which both parties can gain
by war. The French have imitated us (in their financial system); let us, through them imitate ourselves; ourselves in
our better and happier days."

So determined was the demand of the people, Burke went
on, that retrenchment had become a matter of necessity, not
of choice. The Parliament needed only to consider "the best
time and manner of yielding what it is impossible to keep."
While the people were clamoring for "hot reformations,"
Burke declared that he wished to be "a fair mediator between government and the people." He did not favor a plan
to tax placeholders, for that would work a hardship upon
those who really earn their salaries, while it failed to elimi-

nate the sinecures. He courted support by picturing himself as the champion of gradual and equitable reform against the radicals who would sweep out all court officers. Also concili-atory was his contention that "Our ministers are far from wholly to blame for the present ill order which prevails." He recognized the extreme difficulty of "reforming with equity," hence laid down seven basic principles which would govern all his elimination or curtailment of places.

He then proceeded to describe offices which he would abolish with a gentle humor which exposed their ridiculous-ness without wounding the sensibilities of the placeholders. He described "the perpetual virtual adjournment, and the unbroken sitting vacation" of the board of trade. He called it "a sort of gently ripening hothouse, where eight members of Parliament receive salaries of a thousand a year, for a cer-tain given time, in order to mature, at a proper season, a claim to two thousand, granted for doing less and on the credit of having toiled so long in that inferior, laborious de-partment." He declared that "In a job it was conceived and in a job its mother brought it forth." Not even his patent exaggeration could prevent the members of the board from laughing at themselves. Edward Gibbon, the historian of the Roman Empire, who was a member of the board, is reported to have listened to this part of Burke's speech with tears of laughter streaming down his cheeks. In describing this speech *in his Autobiography*, Gibbon said:

"I can never forget the delight with which that diffusive and ingenious orator, Mr. Burke, was heard by all sides of the house, and even by those whose existence he proscribed. The Lords of Trade blushed at their insignificancy, and Mr. Eden's appeal to the two thousand five hundred volumes of our Reports served only to excite a general laugh. . . . But it must be allowed that our duty was not intolerably severe, and that I enjoyed many days and weeks of repose, without being called away from my library to the office.

In the subsequent voting upon individual portions of Burke's bill, the board of trade was abolished by a vote of 207 to 199.

Burke also pointed his gentle sarcasm at the fiction by which the King held various titles in different parts of his kingdom, receiving an ample salary with each title. Why not, Burke asked, retain the King in "his true, simple, undisguised, native character of majesty?" Ridiculing the continuance of the feudal practise of appointing lords to nominal household positions, Burke declared, "The Duke of Warwick's soups, I fear, were not the better for the dignity of his kitchen." The political dangers in these appointments were considerable. "The gorging of a royal kitchen may stint and famish the negotiations of a kingdom." The evils of the state were multiplied—"because the King's turnspit was a member of Parliament." "The good works," he pointed out, of the Board of Works, "are as carefully concealed as other good works ought to be; they are perfectly invisible." In demonstrating the confusion of the treasury accounts, he said, "Death, indeed, domineers over everything but the forms of the exchequer."

Having at once amused the House and demonstrated the undeniable absurdities, expense, and danger of the multitude of sinecures, Burke turned his attention to the more difficult task of allaying the fears and self-interest of the place-holders whose votes he must win. He knew that his reform must be limited by prudential considerations. "I do not propose," he told them, ". . . to take away any pensions." "What the law respects shall be sacred to me." But he appealed to their sense of values higher than their own advantage. "Individuals pass like shadows; but the commonwealth is fixed and stable." Let the question be settled upon terms of true public interest. There must always be a system of pensions for the reward of great services. "There is a time when the weather-beaten vessels of the state ought to come into harbour." Nor would he try to circumscribe these grants too closely. "I am not possessed of an exact common measure between real service and its reward. . . . The service of the public is a thing which cannot be put to auction and struck down to those who will agree to execute it the cheapest." Not parsimony, but order is what he most desired. "But that part of my plan, sir, upon which I principally rest," Burke declared, "that on which I rely for the purpose of binding up, and securing the whole, is to establish a fixed and invariable order in all its payments which it shall not be permitted to the first lord of the treasury, upon any pretence whatsoever, to depart from."

Thus was his plan proposed. It was not carried at once. But Lord North did not feel able after this presentation to oppose it personally, and Parliament considered the scheme for several months. The following February it was again introduced, and provided the occasion for Pitt's first parliamentary speech. In the next year, 1782, when the second Rockingham government was formed, Burke succeeded in putting his plan into operation. Among the abuses which he abolished was a considerable irregular profit formerly attached to his own new office as paymaster of the armed forces. It can, of course, hardly be maintained that this reform was accomplished by the speech which has just been examined. This was only the first of a long series of speeches on the bill. But it contains the heart of Burke's argument, and illustrates the persuasive methods he used to further it. It is a grand speech, of which only a dim idea can be conveyed by the few sentences quoted. It deserves to be known much more widely than it is. It is in many ways the best example of Burke's persuasive technique.

As has been illustrated, Burke's two general methods were conciliation and attack. It should be added that for both of them his great aim was to create a vivid impression. In his many explanations, illustrations, examples, analogies, images, and in the close relationship which he always maintained between general principles and specific instances, he seems to have been convinced that vivid conception induces belief. Perhaps he carried this theory too far, and tended to drown his arguments in a sea of illustrations, so that to his auditors he did not seem to be sufficiently argumentative. But this article of his faith is at least a guarantee that his orations are never dull reading, and never sterile.

Toward the end of his life, especially after the outbreak of the French Revolution, Burke's conciliatory manner almost disappeared, and his use of invective and attack became completely dominant. This fact gives curious interest to a letter which he wrote after his retirement from Parliament to his friend, Mrs. Crewe:

"For a year past, and longer, I have done so much as ever man did to bring and to keep people together. But I have been unfortunate. All the means of conciliation I have used have become so many causes of contention. In that contention, I am certain, I have had no intentional share — as certain as that I have had my full share of punishment. . . . I am little disposed to attack others, and not much more so to defend myself. I have lived, and now I have nothing to do but to die."

Chapter 12—The Debater

Fox's greatest debating weapon was his air of personal candor and sincerity. It is true that during the fight over his East India Bill, during the Regency battle, and during the French Revolution, there were many slanderous stories in circulation of his corrupt and ruthless ambition. But his whole manner of delivery, stumbling at first, then gaining in fluency, and finally rushing along until he became in places almost incoherent, as he was swept by the current of his own powerful feelings, was a guarantee of sincerity to his auditors, and was accepted by them as such. This very depth of feeling was also one of his greatest handicaps, for it hurried him on into storms of denunciation which aroused stubborn resistance in those he attacked. It also induced him often to overstate his feelings in the heat of debate, thus creating an impression which he would later be forced to contradict.

A good example of his pressing, denunciatory, unremitting attack is exhibited in the report of his speech on December 3, 1775, attacking Lord North's bill to prohibit trade with the rebellious colonies. The following paragraph comprises the entire report of his speech, which, doubtless, is merely the stenographer's summary of what he actually said. Thus the arguments are telescoped together, but by that very fact the argumentative method he used becomes clearly apparent.

"I have always given it as my opinion," he said, "that the war now carrying on against the Americans is unjust; but, admitting it to be a just war, admitting that it is practicable, I insist that the means made use of, are not such as will obtain the end. I shall confine myself singly to this ground, and show that this Bill, like every other measure, proves the want of policy, the folly and madness, of the present ministers. I was in great hopes, that they had seen their error, and had given over coercion, and the idea of carrying on war against America by means of acts of Parliament. In order to induce the Americans to submit to your legislature, you pass laws against them, cruel and tyrannical in the extreme. If they complain of one law, your answer to their complaint, is to pass another more rigorous than the former. But they are in rebellion, you say; if so, treat them as rebels are wont to be treated. Send out your fleets and armies against them, and subdue them; but let them have no reason to complain of your laws. Show them, that your laws are mild, just, and equitable, that they therefore are in the wrong, and deserve the punishment they meet with. The very contrary of this has been your wretched policy. I have ever understood it as a first principle, that in rebellion you punish the individuals, but spare the country; but in a war against the enemy, it is your policy to spare the individuals, and lay waste the country. This last has been invariably your conduct against America. I suggested this to you, when the Boston Port Bill was passed. I advised you to find out the offending persons, and to punish them; but what did you do instead of this? You laid the whole town of Boston under terrible contribution, punishing the innocent with the guilty. You answer, that you could not come at the guilty. This very answer shows how unfit, how unable you are, to govern America. If you are forced to punish the innocent to come at the guilty, your government there is, and ought to be, at an end. But, by the bill now before us, you not only punish those innocent persons who are unfortunately mixed with the guilty in North America, but you punish and starve whole islands of unoffending people, unconnected with, and separated from them. Hitherto the Americans have separated the right of taxation from your legislative authority; although they have denied the former, they have acknowledged the latter. This bill will make them deny the one as well as the other. 'What signifies,' they say, 'your giving up the right of taxation, if you are to enforce your legislative authority in the manner you do. This legislative authority so enforced, will at any time coerce taxation, and take from us whatever you see fit to demand.' "

The best examples of how Fox's enthusiasm and deep feeling cause him to use exaggeration in presenting his position might be drawn from his speeches on the American war, from the Regency battle, or from his more choleric speeches on the Fench war.

Probably the one having the most significance in his career, however, occurred March 3, 1782, when Fox supported North's Ministry in a motion for peace with America. "But in so doing," he said as paraphased by the parliamentary reporter, "he desired it might be understood that he did not mean to have any connection with them: from the moment when he should make any terms with one of them, he would rest satisfied to be called the most infamous of mankind; he could not for an instant think of a coalition with men, who, in every public and private transaction, as ministers, had shown themselves void of every principle of honour and honesty; in the hands of such men he would not trust his honour, even for a minute." However, less than a year later, on February 17, 1783, Fox found himself faced by the unpalatable task of explaining to the house how he had come to form a coalition with that very North, whom he had so excoriated. Under the circumstances the coalition may have been proper, but Fox was hard put to it to discover sufficiently plausible rationalizations with which to explain his about-face.

"I am accused," he said, "of having formed a junction with a noble person, whose principles I have been in the habit of opposing for the last

seven years of my life. . . . That I shall have the honour of concurring
with the noble lord in the the blue ribbon on the present question is very
certain; and if men of honour can meet on points of general national concern, I see no reason for calling such a meeting an unnatural junction. It is
neither wise nor noble to keep up animosities for ever. It is neither just
nor candid to keep up animosity when the cause of it is no more. It is not
in my nature to bear malice, or to live in ill-will. My friendships are perpetual, my enmities are not so. . . . When a man ceases to be what he was,
when the opinions which made him obnoxious are changed, he then is no
more my enemy, but my friend. The American war, and the American
question is at an end. The noble lord has profited from fatal experience.
While that system was maintained, nothing could be more asunder than the
noble lord and myself. But it is now no more; and it is therefore wise and
candid to put an end also to the ill will, the animosity, the rancour, and
the feuds which it occasioned. I am free to acknowledge that when I was
the friend of the noble lord in the blue ribbon, I found him open and sincere; when the enemy, honourable and manly. I never had reason to say of
the noble lord in the blue ribbon, that he practised any of those little subterfuges, tricks, and stratagems which I found in others; any of those behind-hand and paltry manoeuvres which destroy confidence between human beings, and degrade the character of the statesman and the man."

Now Fox was doubtless sincere in both of these speeches,
but both of his conclusions could hardly be true. He was
impelled into exaggeration by the enthusiasm of the moment. It remained a characteristic quality of his argumentative style.

Like Burke, he did not rely entirely upon denunciation
and attack. But he was not very successful at conciliation.
He partially at least supplied its place by his frequent
practise of stating the arguments of his opponents with
full fairness, sometimes better than they had done themselves, and then by restatement and re-interpretation drawing opposite conclusions from the same facts they had used.
This practise gave an air of fairness and of logical impenetrability to his attack. A good example of this practise

appears in his speech of April 20, 1791, on abolishing the slave trade. After re-stating the argument of the West Indies planters that slaves must be imported, for they die faster than they breed, Fox cried, "What, then, was the purpose for which this accursed and horrid traffic in human creatures was desired to be kept up? The purpose was this —in order to give the planters the opportunity of destroying the negroes on their estates, as fast as they pleased." Another example comes in his condemnation of the treason and sedition laws, on May 23, 1797. "You tell the people, that when everything goes well, when they are happy and comfortable, then they may meet freely, to recognize their happiness, and pass eulogiums on their government; but that in a moment of war and calamity . . . it is not permitted them to meet together, because then . . . they might think proper to condemn ministers. What a mockery is this! What an insult."

Fox also secured an air of fairness by his direct appeals to the judgment of his auditors, asking them what they would do if the vote were not a question of ministerial support. One illustration, from his speech of February 3, 1800, urging peace with France, will suffice to show his method in using this device.

"Sir, what is the question this night? We are called upon to support ministers in refusing a frank, candid, and respectful offer of negotiation, and to countenance them in continuing the war. Now, I would put the question in another way. Suppose ministers had been inclined to adopt the line of conduct which they pursued in 1796 and 1797, and that to-night, instead of a question on a war address, it had been an address to his majesty, to thank him for accepting the overture, and to open a negotiation to treat for peace: I ask the gentlemen opposite—I appeal to the whole 558 representatives of the people—to lay their hands upon their hearts, and to say whether they would not have cordially voted for such an address? Would they, or would they not? Yes, Sir, if the address had breathed a spirit of peace, your benches would have resounded with rejoicings, and with praises of a measure that was likely to bring back the blessings of tranquility. On the present occasion, then, I ask for the vote of none but of those who, in the secret confession of their conscience, admit, at this instant, while they hear me, that they would have cheerfully and heartily voted with the minister for an address directly the reverse of this."

Perhaps the best view of Fox's persuasive methods can be obtained by tracing them through the course of one of his outstanding speeches.   For this purpose a good speech to use is that of March 1, 1792, in which he demanded a vote of censure against Pitt for having armed against Russia in the course of a diplomatic dispute over the town of Oczakow.   The previous year, Fox had undoubtedly prevented Pitt from hurling England into an unwise, unnecessary and ruinous war.   In this speech, he is triumphing over his adversary in a speech which Lord Brougham described as "perhaps the ablest, and certainly the most characteristic, of all Mr. Fox's productions."

Fox's speech came as the climax of a long and galling attack by a succession of Whig orators, alternated with defences of Pitt's conduct by his colleagues.   Pitt himself remained silent, and Dundas called upon Fox to speak, in order that Pitt might be allowed the last word, for it was a rule of the House that no member could speak twice in the same debate.   Fox responded to the call, but objected to it as improper to allow Pitt the last speech, when he might make an extravagant statement without fear of contradiction.   Fox pointed out that Pitt ought to have consented to a discussion of the question in a committee of the whole, when any member might speak as often as he wished.

"If the right honourable gentleman is truly desirous of meeting the charges against him, and has confidence in his ability to vindicate his conduct, why not pursue the course which would be manly and open?" But "to confess the truth, never did man stand so much in need of every advantage!" Fox then reviewed the facts that during the debates of the previous session, Pitt had consistently refused to tell Parliament the cause of the armament, on the grounds that to publish that information would encumber the negotiation. However, after the negotiation had failed, he still refused to place complete information in their hands, and challenged them to prove him guilty. Now Pitt asserted by implication, said Fox, "I will make a speech, which you shall not have an opportunity to contradict, and I will throw myself on my majority, that make you dumb forever." After some examination and rejection of the arguments that the armament was needed to maintain the balance of power in Europe, Fox constructed an ingenious dilemma for the ministry. "If, therefore, it was so important to recover Oczakow, it is not recovered, and ministers ought to be censured. If unimportant, they ought to be censured for-arming; but if so important as they have stated it, they ought to be censured for disarming without having gotten it." He then ridiculed the only method of escape from the dilemma.

"But they tell us it is unfair to involve them in this dilemma. There was a middle course to be adopted. Oczakow was certainly of much importance; but this importance was to be determined upon by circumstances. Sir, we are become nice, indeed, in our political arithmetic. . . . Thus it seems that Oczakow was worth an armament, but not worth a war; it was worth a threat, but not worth carrying that threat into execution! Sir, I can conceive nothing so degrading and dishonourable as such an argument. To hold out a menace without ever seriously meaning to enforce it, constitutes, in common language, the true description of a bully. Applied to the transactions of a nation, the disgrace is deeper, and the consequences fatal to its honor."

"How do ministers think on this subject? Oczakow was everything by itself; but when they added to Oczakow the honor of England, it became nothing! Oczakow by itself, threatened the balance of Europe. Oczakow and national honor united weighed nothing in the scale! Honor is, in their political arithmetic, a *minus* quantity, to be subtracted from the value of Oczakow!"

Fox then constructed another dilemma. The ministers had asserted that the reason they did not proceed with the armament to the point of war was that public opinion forbade it. But they should have ascertained public opinion before they engaged the honor of England by threatening war; they should have laid all of the facts before Parliament and obtained the opinion of that body. As a matter of fact, they had demanded the support of their majority as a matter of confidence, without explaining the issue involved in the armament. Such being true, they ought to abide the consequences of having on their own responsibility proceeded directly contrary to public opinion, as they admitted doing, and resign. Fox then tried to separate Pitt's majority from him, pointing out that it had been insulted by his demand of mere subservient voting, with no explanation of the measure which was voted on. He imagined Pitt addressing his majority, assuring them that he had sought for public expressions of opinion, and had listened to the minority opposition. But "as to you, my trusty majority, I neglected you! I had other business for you! It is not your office to give opinions; your business is to confide!" Fox next called attention to a statement made by Dundas, which he interpreted as an admission that the minority had prevailed upon the ministry to refrain from war. "Let me," said Fox, "indulge the satisfaction of reflecting, that though we have not the emoluments of office, nor the patronage of power, yet we are not excluded from great influence on the measures of government." A little later he made his first direct attack upon Pitt.

A parallel but superior attack on Lord North's policy occurred in Fox's speech of February 19, 1778, when he was in the very height of his powers as a speaker: "The noble lord hoped and was disappointed. He expected a great deal, and found little to answer his expectations. He thought America would have submitted to his laws, and they resisted them. He thought they would have submitted to his armies, and they were beaten by inferior numbers. He made conciliatory propositions, and he thought they would succeed, but they were rejected. He appointed commissioners to make peace, and he thought they had powers, but he found they could not make peace, and nobody believed that they had any powers." Incidentally, the grammatical errors in this passage are, his contemporaries agree, typical of Fox. They emphasize the thoroughly extempore character of his address – his dependence upon manner of delivery, rather than niceties of style, to give effectiveness to his matter.

"What, therefore, was the right claimed by the right honourable gentleman to enter into this dispute? I will answer. The right of a proud man, anxious to play a lofty part. France had gone off the stage. The character of the miserable disturber of empires was vacant, and he resolved to boast and vapor, and play his antic tricks and gestures on the same theater. . . .

"And what was the end? Why, that after pledging the King's name in the most deliberate and solemn manner; after lofty vaporing, menacing, promising, denying, turning, and turning again . . . the right honourable gentleman crouches humbly at her (Russia's) feet; entreats, submissively supplicates of her moderation, that she will grant him some small trifle of what he asks, if it is but by way of a boon; and finding at last that he can get nothing, either by threats or his prayers, gives up the whole precisely as she insisted upon having it!"

Fox again tried to interpose a wedge between Pitt and his majority, by declaring that Pitt so divided the executive and legislative functions that,

"he has reserved for himself the higher and more respectable share of the business, and leaves all the dirty work to us. Is he asked why the House of Commons made the armament last year? He answers, The House of Commons did not make the armament! I made it. The House of Commons only approved of it. Is he asked why he gave up the object of the armament, after he had made it? I did not give it up! he exclaims. . . . It is the House of Commons that gives it up! . . . It is to this House that you must look for the shame and guilt of your disgrace. To himself he takes the more conspicuous character of menacer. It is he that distributes provinces, and limits empires; while he leaves to this House the humbler office of licking the dust, and begging forgiveness."

Fox then carried the discussion through a lengthy examination of the state of Europe, to demonstrate that there was no necessity of the armament to swing the balance of power in Europe toward a favorable settlement of the dispute between Turkey and Russia. This is perhaps the most substantial portion of his speech, but inasmuch as the arguments involve lengthy trains of reasoning, it is the portion least amenable to quotation. Probably for this reason, Fox is often judged by the quotable invective in his speeches, rather than by the unquotable logic. Perhaps that logic may be taken for granted, as no statesman could have gained the influence exercised through a small minority, which Fox exerted, had he not been upheld by the unquestionable logic of facts.

But, he was too astute to let the facts speak for themselves. He pressed his conclusions unrelentingly upon his auditors. The conclusion he reached from the facts of this speech was that Pitt sacrificed his country to his ambition. "Let him keep but his place, he cares not what else he loses. With other men, reputation and glory are the objects of ambition; power and place are coveted, but as the means of these. For the minister, power and place are sufficient of themselves. With them he is content; for them he can calmly sacrifice every proud distinction that ambition covets, and every noble prospect to which it points the way!"

From this speech, have been cited several examples of Fox's frequently used device of imagining what his opponents must say if they spoke logically according to their acts, and quoting them upon this basis. It is one method of reducing their position to the absurd. Also noted has been the chief justification for his denunciatory style of debate— that he aimed the denunciation solely at the ministers, and tried thereby to destroy the majority's confidence in them. Perhaps, this was a wise alternative to the only other course, one of conciliating the ministers and thus persuading them to adopt his views. The latter method of compromise, concession, patience, and humiliating acceptance of an inferior position was contrary to Fox's deepest nature. If followed, it might have resulted eventually in his loss of prestige, and in the destruction of the nascent liberal movement in politics. The facts, however, would seem to indicate otherwise. Certainly on two major issues, parliamentary reform and abolition of the slave trade, Fox's rejection of proposals for gradual reforms postponed both benefits for decades. Responsibility for the rejection of Dundas's proposed slave trade compromise, however, rests fully as much upon Pitt as the minister and upon the leaders in the House of Lords as upon Fox.

Among Fox's other leading persuasive devices, one he often invoked was an establishment of his prestige. This he accomplished chiefly by citing previous instances in which his predictions had been justified, and, ultimately, accepted by the ministry. It was a frequent method used by both Fox and Burke during the American war, when it was most true, and used by Fox often during the French war. That device had the merit that it could not very well be abused. It was clearly an appeal to admitted facts. It had the weakness, of course, that having been right on a previous question does not give assurance that one will be right on a new problem, concerning which only the ministry could be in possession of all the facts. History, however, has borne out Fox's contention that he was right much of the time, and that Pitt would have done well to heed him.

A savage, ironic type of humor was also used by Fox in displaying the absurdity of his opponents' position. His attack upon Lord George Germain, on December 2, 1777, in the debate on the bill prohibiting trade with the American colonies, is an excellent illustration.

"For the two years that a certain noble lord has presided over American affairs, the most violent, scalping, tomahawk measures have been pursued: bleeding has been his only prescription. If a people deprived of their ancient rights are grown tumultuous,—bleed them! If they are attacked with a spirit of insurrection,—bleed them! If their fever should rise into rebellion,—bleed them, cries this state physician! more blood! more blood! still more blood! When Dr. Sangrado had persevered in a similar practise of bleeding his patients,—killing by the very means which he adopted as a cure,—his man took the liberty to remonstrate upon the necessity of relaxing in a practise to which thousands of their patients had fallen sacrifices, and which was beginning to bring their names into disrepute. The Doctor answered, 'I believe we have, indeed, carried the matter a little too far, but you must know I have written a book upon the efficacy of this practise; therefore, though every patient we have should die by it, we must continue the bleeding for the credit of my book'."

In addition to illustrating Fox's argument by ironic humor, this citation also shows his skillful use of analogy. This latter device he often used. Another illustrative example is found during the debate on Burke's reform bill, on February 8, 1780. Fox proposed bringing the matter at once to the test of a vote, and deciding the issue in the same manner as Solomon decided between the two women claiming to be mothers of the disputed child, ". . . see who will father this dear but denied child, Corruption!"

His use of emotional appeals to seal his arguments is well illustrated in his speeches favoring abolition of the slave trade. Speaking on two consecutive days, he first denounced the "hard hearts" and "inaccessible understandings" that could vote for a continuance of proved evils. Then he proceeded to such descriptions of the cruelties practised on the negroes who were captured in the African jungles that the members shrank aghast from the recital. Fox drove his point home with relentless insistence. "Will the House, then," said he, "sanction enormities, the bare recital of which was sufficient to make them shudder? Let them first remember that humanity consisted not in a squeamish ear. It consisted not in starting or shrinking at such tales as these, but in a disposition of heart to relieve misery, and to prevent the repetition of cruelty."

Fox possessed that gift without which little else matters in debate—the ability to so marshal and arrange his facts as to give them their greatest possible weight. His intellectual facility in this respect was out of all proportion to his mere stylistic ability in polishing his words. This was his greatest merit as a persuasive speaker.

Chapter 13 – The Wit

Sheridan was not a master of conciliatory argument in the usual sense, but he supplied that deficiency with his skill at bringing the house into good humor, and thus disarming antagonism. This, however, was his occasional, rather than his constant practise. Like Burke and Fox, he possessed two very dissimilar methods. His other, and commoner one was direct and severe attack, belittling and ridiculing the arguments of his opponents. Under this latter method he developed a wide variety of ways in which to depreciate the character or credit of his opponents. The following charges against his adversaries are made so often as to be considered among his typical persuasive devices: inconsistency, corruption, desire for arbitrary power, ignorance, deliberate falsehood, stupidity, betrayal of the rights of the people, failure to understand the English character, misrepresentation of their opponents' arguments, avoidance of the question, "railroading" bills through rapidly without giving the opposition an opportunity to examine them, insincerity, over-riding the rights of Parliament, and failure to understand human nature.

These attacks upon the characters of his opponents are balanced throughout his speeches with defences of his own character, based upon the following considerations: his sincerity, his consistency, his friendliness toward the people, his dependence upon facts and logical arguments, and his readiness to sacrifice his own well-being for the good of the public.

In addition to attacking his opponents and defending himself, other general characteristics may be noted as part of his persuasive technique. Facts, figures, precedents, letters, and reports are cited rather sparingly by Sheridan. The use of these demanded a type of close research which was distasteful to him. For instance, in his reply to Lord Mornington, he admitted that he had not taken time to read the pamphlet upon which much of the discussion turned. He was content to accept Lord Mornington's version of it. Ridicule, sarcasm, depreciation and invective he used very liberally. Analogies, hypothetical cases and specific instances to support his general charges against the ministry were also freely used. These were particularly congenial to his poetic imagination. He used dilemmas to about the same extent as Fox, and rather more than Burke. He persisted in his practise of interpreting the words and arguments of his opponents to favor his own side of the case—a method that might be supposed weak, since the audience would know that a real difference of opinion did exist. His appeals to patriotism, and to the rights of the people were frequent. His use of the *reductio ad absurdum* was frequently exercised in conjunction with rhetorical exaggeration, which weakened its effectiveness. Rhetorical questions were used by him very freely to emphasize his points and bring them closely home to his auditors.

An excellent example of argument by means of rhetorical questions is found in Sheridan's speech on the Failure of the Helder invasion into Holland, delivered on February 10, 1800.

"From being our allies they (the Dutch) became our enemies," he said. "But previous to this change, what were the symptoms of cordiality and good understanding when we were endeavoring to defend Holland? Did not our troops leave that country, complaining of the people, irritated by the reproaches? After the success of the French invasion, was our conduct calculated to increase the number of our friends, and to diminish the number of our enemies? Was it right, after the Stadholder had taken refuge in this country, to consider him as sovereign of Holland, which he never was, (and) to require his consent to the seizure of so much Dutch property? Were such measures conciliatory? Did they tend to promote the interest of the Stadholder? In the negotiation for peace at Lisle, what was the conduct of ministers? . . . What were the Dutch to think of this proceeding? Smarting under the losses they had sustained, must they not have considered us as gross hypocrites when lately we affected such a zeal for their interests, which in the instances alluded to, we had rendered so much subservient to our own?"

His ability to wield stinging sarcasm with terrible effectiveness was well demonstrated in his attack on Pitt, March 7, 1788. In the debate on Pitt's East India Bill, when the feeling over the Regency dispute was still intense, Sheridan said of Pitt:

"His friends talked much of his conscience; and, fruitful in excuses for the errors of his system, never failed to say, that he was debauched into every iniquity and folly that he committed. An honourable gentleman speaking of him, had said, that in his bill he was sure that his conscience had been surprised. It was bad advice, and not wicked intention, from which this bill had originated. He was not unwilling to give ear to this apology. He hoped it was true, and he partly believed it. He did not hesitate in agreeing with his admirers, that he had people about him very capable of leading him wrong. It was his original crime that he had connected himself with those from whom no good counsel could come; and lamenting, as they all must do, the consequences of his want of vigilance, and the misfortunes of his connections, it was earnestly to be wished, that his conscience would either keep a better look-out, or that he would keep better company."

Typically Sheridanian is the rapier stroke of humor rather than the bludgeoning of direct attack. This is the kind of blow which it is impossible to side-step and very difficult to resist. Judging from contemporary accounts, it would appear that no other member of Parliament could approach Sheridan in this department of oratory, although Lord North at an earlier day had probably been as skillful in witty repartee. But there is no aspect of speech which is so evanescent and fleeting as humor. So much depends on the delicacy of the gesture, the flash of the eye, the inflection of the voice, the mood of the audience, and so little on the actual spoken word. Hence, many of Sheridan's best jests seem flat and stale to us today. His wit is best preserved in the playful satire, often merging into the severe, with which he punctured the claims of the ministry. Many passages of this sort sprinkle his speeches. One, which is sufficient to show his light and deft touch, occurs in the course of his previously cited speech on the failure of the Helder invasion of Holland, delivered on February 10, 1800. Nothing, Sheridan asserted, had been gained but a few old Dutch ships.

"But I see," he said, "by the gestures of the right honourable gentlemen opposite, that they are of the opinion that the Dutch fleet is not the only thing we have gained. It may be so, to be sure, in a certain way. It was an expedition of discovery, and not altogether unsuccessful in that view. We have made three notable discoveries:—we have, in the first place, discovered that there is no reliance to be placed in the Chancellor of the Exchequer's knowledge of human nature; we have discovered, that

Holland is a country intersected by dykes, ditches and canals; and we have discovered, that their weather there too, is not so good in October as it is in June! . . . This information, however, may be purchased too dear: if we consider the number of lives which have been lost; if we reflect that the tenth of every man's income has been squandered, that so much of our best blood has been shed in vain, and all by the best conduct of ministers, we shall have little reason to boast that our discoveries have been easily made, and our acquisitions cheaply purchased. . . .

"We tell the Dutch to 'Forget and forgive the past.' But, how will they understand this advice? Will they not consider it as a recommendation to *forget* that they ever had colonies, and to *forgive* us for taking them? . . . If, instead of all the fine reflections upon religion, social order, and their former government, he (Pitt) had said we will give you back all your colonies, the argument would have been understood, and the effect might have been favorable."

To fully encompass the debating methods of Sheridan, it is necessary to follow him through the course of an entire speech and note the arguments and devices he used. For this purpose his speech on the Army Estimates, December 8, 1802, will serve. It is particularly interesting for in it Sheridan reversed all his previous diatribes against the French war, and urged that (after the brief truce following the peace of Amiens) the war be renewed. It is easy to see why such a speech was made. Pitt was temporarily out of power, and Addington was prime minister. Addington was never very strongly entrenched, and at this time he was obviously weakening under the attacks of the pacifist Foxites on one side, and the war party led by Pitt on the other. Sheridan believed that the only way to save the Addington government, and thus to keep Pitt, his inveterate enemy, from power, was to precipitate the war anew while Addington was still at the helm. It is very doubtful if even this ruse could have kept Pitt from returning to office. At any rate, it seems to be the underlying explanation for this speech.

In his introduction, Sheridan professed a reluctance to

speak, inasmuch as he would have to disagree with the peace favoring majority. However, he said, we all agree on the tremendous importance of the occasion, and we all have a right to know what the ministry is doing; the crisis should raise us all above mere party feelings.

Commencing the main thread of his argument, he declared in favor of increasing the army because of the French attack upon Switzerland; the danger was obvious. He agreed with a previous speaker who warned against making any pledges to allies, for in the last war the late ministry (Pitt's) broke all the pledges that were made. He ridiculed the argument that the army ought not to be increased lest France think England were becoming fearful. "If we vote no force," he pointed out, "an enemy will know we have none . . . Sir," he continued, "when every house in my neighborhood has been attacked and robbed by a gang of ruffians, how my having no arms is to save me from a visit from them, I must leave the honourable gentleman to explain." A speaker had declared France would have nothing to gain by an invasion of England. Already France controlled Europe and could surely desire nothing more. "It is in our power to measure her territory," Sheridan admitted, ". . . but it is scarcely within the grasp of any man's mind to measure the ambition of Bonaparte. Why, when all Europe bows down before him—why, when he has subdued the whole continent, he should feel such great respect for us, I am at a loss to discover." A speaker had said that Bonaparte's rivalry with England was purely commercial; on the contrary, he knows nothing of commerce—only of war. Bonaparte's specious plea that all Europe is one family must be resisted. "Let us be visiting acquaintance, but I do implore him not to consider us as one of the family.

The war party might look for favor in what I have said, but actually if they were in power they would act no differently from the present ministry." His Majesty's messsage was excellent, for "it satisfied me that a sense of wrong, and a resentment of injury, may live under moderate language." The war party had been hard put to it to discover any grounds for objecting to Addington's government. He came into power at a difficult juncture and had governed well. It was inconsistent for Pitt's friends to demand Pitt's return to power, for Pitt himself has praised the person and the conduct of the present minister. That Pitt is needed by the country is absurd. "Mr. Pitt the only man to save the country! If a nation depends only upon one man, it cannot, and, I will add, it does not deserve to be saved; it can only be done by the Parliament and the people."

Sheridan concluded with a manly assertion of his right to differ with Fox (as he had done most markedly in this speech) when his judgment led him to. At the time it seemed to him that Bonaparte's only utility to England was to make them all love their country more, and to arouse their determination to die, if need be, in England's defence.

This outline, brief as it is, is sufficient to display many of Sheridan's favorite forms of arguments. They were: charges of inconsistency, claims of personal merit and attack on the credit of his adversaries, and an intermingling of humor and ridicule with argument, until it is almost impossible to tell where logic leaves off and sophistry begins. The speech contains sense and nonsense inextricably mixed, and as such it stands as a symbol of Sheridan's parliamentary career. He was a jester who could be terribly in earnest at times. But for his readers now, as for his auditors then, it is sometimes difficult to tell in which character he appeared.

Chapter 14 – The Artisan

Pitt's speaking style was conditioned by the fact that during almost twenty of the twenty-five years he spent in Parliament he was prime minister. His lightest utterance was the official statement of the English government. Under these circumstances his responsibility was tremendous. Fox, Burke, and Sheridan could say what they pleased in the heat of debate—and often they said some very rash things – but in a literal sense, whatever Pitt said would be used against him. Several times he let slip remarks which caused him acute regret. Such also was a haughty declaration which slipped into his speech just before North's resignation, in March, 1782. Pitt was not yet twenty-three years old, he was aligned with no one of the strong political groups in Parliament, he had only been in that body for a little more than one session. Yet, to his own astonishment he heard himself saying, "For myself, I could not expect to form part of a new administration: but were my doing so more within my reach, I feel myself bound to declare that I never would accept a subordinate position." He sat down feeling

that he would almost rather have bitten off his tongue than
have uttered these words. They caused a flurry of incredu-
lous astonishment through the House. Truly, the younger
Pitt lacked nothing of the arrogance of the elder. This
pride remained with him as one of his oustanding charac-
eristics throughout life.

But, if Pitt needed to be particularly careful to curb rash
utterances, he could not do so by refusing to speak. One of
the chief reasons he obtained and held the prime minister-
ship was the fact that he was practically the only man who
had the courage and the ingenuity to defend the government policies against the continuous and determined opposition of the great Whigs. His Tory following was prede-
termined to vote for the government measures. Nonetheless,
he had to provide the rationalizations by which they justified
their votes.

Placed in such a position, there were two things which
Pitt needed to do, and he did both of them exceedingly
well. He had to be able to make difficult policies instantly
clear to the uninformed and often bleared minds of the
Tory squires. This was particularly true of his budget
speeches, in which he sought to win their support for new
taxes, and for reorganization of the old revenue system.
Launching forth, thus, upon new ground, Pitt could not
afford to take his majority vote for granted. He discovered
upon the questions of parliamentary reform, revision of the
Irish commercial treaties, Catholic emancipation, and abolition of the slave trade that his following was subservient to
the King rather than to him. Where his policy was not
clearly along orthodox lines, it aroused their suspicion, and
possible dissent. In introducing his measures, then, Pitt took
great pains to be easily and clearly understood. But in ad-

dition, when he was defending his administration against attack, it was often desirable for Pitt not be understood. Just so surely as the keen analysis of the Foxites found the weak spots in his administration, he must spread a screen of dissimulation around the issues to prevent his followers from understanding the course of the debate. Hence Pitt became the master of two styles: one clear, logical and direct; the other wordy, diffuse and empty.

When he used the latter, his intent was simply to confuse the issue; he hoped to be "sufficiently obscure to sound convincing." The direct and forthright presentation of irrelevancies; a circuitous approach to the problem, as though he meant to take a "broad" view of the subject, when in reality he merely skirted it; and an eager and exhaustive discussion of such relevant but unessential elements of the question as helped to further his arguments—these methods may all be observed in his speeches when he was defending his administration against strong attacks. This obscure style may be considered as one general type of persuasion which Pitt employed.

Most of his speeches were clear, fluent and "copious," in which he presented facts colored by his interpretation, but with a strong appearance of fairness and lack of bias. Among his favorite devices to accomplish this impression should be mentioned amplification, re-interpretation, and appeal to practicality. Amplification of ideas is very frequent in his speeches. It takes some such form as in the following sentence, in which he declares, ". . . . there is no extremity of war, there is no extremity of honourable contest, that is not preferable to the name and pretence of peace, which must be in reality a disgraceful capitulation, a base, an abject surrender of everything that constitutes the pride, the safety, and happiness of England." By such means, he gave the impression of saying a great deal more than he did say, and invested his subject with an emphatic degree of importance.

An example of his method of re-interpretation of an opponent's argument presents itself in the speech on the French Negotiations for Peace. In replying to Sir John Sinclair, Pitt said, "But let not the honourable baronet imagine there is any ground for his apprehension, that by adopting the language of the address, which ascribes the continuance of the war to the ambition of the enemy, we shall declare a system of endless animosity between the nations of Great Britain and France. I say directly the contrary. He who scruples to declare, that in the present moment the government of France are acting as much in contradiction to the known wishes of the French nation, as to the just pretensions and anxious wishes of the people of Great Britain—he who scruples to declare them the authors of this calamity, deprives us of the consolatory hope which we are inclined to cherish, of some future change of circumstances more favourable to our wishes." The appeal to practicality ran through and was a basic part of nearly all of Pitt's speeches. A convenient illustration may be abstracted from his speech on the necessity of preparing for war with France, on February 1, 1793:

"We owe our present happiness and prosperity, which has never been equalled in the annals of mankind, to a mixture of monarchical government. We feel and know we are happy under that form of government. . . . The equity of our laws, and the freedom of our political system, have been the envy of every surrounding nation. In this country no man, in consequences of his riches or rank, is so high as to be above the reach of the laws, and no individual is so poor or inconsiderable as not to be within their protection."

As prime minister, Pitt was a central target for all the virulent attacks which his opponents wished to make upon him. Far from granting him immunity, his office gave *carte blanche* to all who wished to indulge in political abuse. All final governmental responsibility rested upon him. All failures were attributed to him. All political ambition of the opposition members depended upon success in unseating him. Hence attacks were constant, and a large portion of Pitt's persuasive technique was composed of devices for turning or repelling them.

Naturally, he often converted his defence into an attack. This practise is well illustrated in his reply to a severe attack by Sheridan, on May 30, 1794:

". . . it will be allowed, with respect to the honourable gentleman, that he is possessed of such ingenuity as to bring together every argument, however incongruous, that may suit his purpose, and give it an appearance of connection with the question. What then was the amount of his arguments? That you ought to discontinue the war, because it afforded the means of fabricating plots in this county. The honourable gentleman thought proper, without the smallest regard either to probability or decency, to assert, that plots had been fabricated, and that these plots had no foundation except in the foul imagination of ministers. The abuse of that honourable gentleman has been too often repeated to have any degree of novelty with me, or to be entitled to any degree of importance, either with myself, or any other of my honourable friends, who may occasionally happen to be its objects. But I must own, that there is some degree of novelty indeed in this mode of attack against a report originating from twenty-one members, to whose character for honour and integrity I will not do any injury by comparing it with the quarter from which the attack was made."

At this, Pitt was interrupted by a point of order and a request for an apology, but he was upheld by the Speaker in his assertion that Sheridan's attack had merited such a reply.

If Pitt's position peculiarly exposed him to personal abuse, it served him well in the strategy of debate in at least

three major respects. First of all, it assured him an attentive and respectful hearing whenever he chose to speak.
Sheridan was stating only an obvious fact when he observed
of Pitt, on May 7, 1793, "He knew the advantage which
the right honourable gentleman had in that house, and
that for many reasons, he was more likely to be attended
to than those who were to oppose him; few, if any, were
heard within the walls of that house so attentively as that
right honourable gentleman." Secondly, Pitt was always
enabled to turn any attack by declaring that the opposition
members were only trying to get his place. There was
sufficient truth in this charge to give it plausibility. It became almost the staple of debate during the frenzied contest
following the dismissal of the Fox-North coalition in December, 1783. In the third place, Pitt was always able to
withhold any information which he did not wish to let his
opponents have by declaring it to be a state secret. Fox and
Sheridan were continually complaining against this kind of
treatment. In his speech on the Russian armament, for instance, Fox represented Pitt as saying, "I hear what you
say, I could answer all your charges; but I know my duty
to my King too well to submit, at this moment, to expose
the secrets of state, and to lay the reasons before you of the
measure on which I demand your confidence."

Another of Pitt's peculiarities in debate, which might be
termed a persuasive device, was his fluency of utterance
and uniform earnestness of manner. This manner, at once
monotonous and pleasing, exercised a sort of hypnotic sway
over his listeners. Combined with his positive manner and
the reputation of his family name, it gave him great authority with the people outside of Parliament. There was a
general belief among the English public that Pitt was the

man who could "weather the storm." It was this popular support, combined with that of the King, which doubtless was Pitt's greatest persuasive instrument.

Pitt's speech on the French Negotiations for Peace on November 10, 1797, offers a fair sampling of the persuasive devices and appeals which he employed. The list, of course, would be extended by adding those employed in other speeches, but by itself it indicates considerable versatility. Several devices, such as his identification of himself with the best interests of his audience, restatement of the issues, direct appeal to the fair judgment of those who disagree with him, and the *reductio ad absurdum*, occur numerous times during the course of the speech. Among those which occur only once or twice, the following may be cited: stress on the necessity of unanimity, flattery of opponents, modest rejection of praise, appeal to courage, imputation of war guilt solely to the French leaders, an appeal to documentary evidence, explanation of a "misconception" which has caused his opponents to disagree with him, declaration that his position mediates between the opposite and extreme points of view of his two sets of opponents, explanation of a false dilemma in which his opponents had sought to involve him, destruction of all alternatives to the course he had pursued, relation of instances of his fairness in making concessions to France, use of dialogue to make a point vivid, use of rhetorical questions, and appeal to sentiments of patriotism.

One of Pitt's effective persuasive devices was to point out the consequences of acting upon the proposals of his opponents. An example of this device is taken from his denunciation of the fourteen resolutions designed to end the French war, presented in Fox's speech of May 30, 1794.

"What then do the resolutions, prepared by the right honourable gentleman, call upon you to do? To counteract all your former sentiments—to abandon those principles to which you have pledged yourselves—to rescind the measures which you have solemnly adopted—and, after having displayed the extent of your resources, and put into the hands of his Majesty means for carrying on the war, to tell him that he shall not avail himself of those means, and abandon every resource, except that of making peace with France. It is to require you, at the end of the session, to make a recantation of all that you have done in every former part of it—to contradict all your former professions, and to renounce opinions formed upon a most serious deliberation, and confirmed by repeated acts."

Pitt's methods may best be seen in operation if we follow his persuasive technique through the course of an entire speech. For this purpose, Pitt's brief reply on February 15, 1796, to Grey's motion for a new effort to effect peace will serve admirably. In his introduction, Pitt pointed out the difficulty he was under in speaking on this motion, for his official situation give particular significance to any remarks he might make either favoring or opposing peace. But upon one aspect of the question, he said, there could be little chance of disagreement. "However I may be disposed to favour that object, which the motion seems principally to have in view, I can by no means concede the grounds on which it has been followed up; – I mean that from a view of our situation, and of the events of the war, we should discover such shameful humiliation, such hopeless despondency, as to abandon every thing for which we have formerly contended, and be disposed to prostrate ourselves at the feet of the enemy." The situation of England was not such as to make it necessary to accept a peace dictated by a conqueror. Indeed, recent successes led to the opinion that sometime in the near future a favorable peace might be secured.

Pitt then directly challenged the heckling maneuvers of his adversaries. "I must protest the practice of being called upon from day to day, from week to week, from time to time, to declare what are precisely our views on the posture of affairs, or what are the steps, which we may think it necessary in consequence to adopt. . . . On a subject so critical, I am afraid lest I should overstep the line of my duty, by entering too much into detail. It is a subject on which it is impossible to descant so minutely as the honourable gentleman seems to expect, without breaking in upon that principle which has guided every discreet minister in treating subjects of this nature." Grey's motion, by calling for a separate peace, would have the immediate effect of dissolving the confederacy against France. This had been precisely the object which the French themselves most eagerly sought; it would be tantamount to making the French the dictators of Europe. It would be impossible to obtain both a speedy and an honourable peace, as Grey's motion requested. "But an honourable peace we may have, if we persevere in the same firm and vigorous line of conduct which we have hitherto pursued." This is certain, from French admissions of "their defective and almost exhausted means for carrying on the war." "On this ground I oppose the motion. If I were not sincerely, and anxiously desirous of peace, I should be forfeiting my duty to the country, and violating the trust which I hold from my public situation; but I can never consent to the proposition of peace, unless the terms should be consistent with our present honour, suitable to our present condition, and compatible with our future security."

Pitt then reminded the house that two months previously it had voted to give ministers power to negotiate a peace,

without binding them in any way as to the time or circumstances of such negotiation. He had said then that it would
be fatal to bind the ministers by explicit directions. "Those
who differ from me in general, and who have thought the
war altogether unnecessary, I did not then, nor do I now,
expect to convince. But the house at large thought as I do."
Now his opponents have accused him of insincerity for not
having used that power to treat. He scorns the imputation.
"I wish ardently for peace—but not for any but an honourable peace." "I do not hold out a prospect of immediate
peace, nor do I state any period that I can ascertain for it;
I only say that it will not be the fault of his Majesty's servants if the period is remote. . . . It all depends on this,
whether the disposition of the enemy shall be more moderate than any we have lately seen of their professions."

The French government, he insisted, had shown no tendency to conciliation, but rather had been industriously
propagating the story that it would grant peace only if England asked for it. "Thus then, we are to have peace if we
shall sue for it; that is, if we shall abandon that for which
our ancestors have fought so bravely. If we shall abandon
our allies; if we shall abandon the safety of all Europe, and
sacrifice to France everything that is dear to us, and offer to
them homage, and grant them an unconditional and uncom-
pensated restitution of all that has been their's, and all that
has been in the possession of those whom they have forced
to be their allies—then, in return for this, they will offer
the people of England their fraternization."

He concluded with a declaration that England need not
fear the results of the war unless by some such motion as
this of Grey's the Parliament should officially declare itself

unwilling and unable to continue the war; ". . . and therefore, as a lover of my country, and of justice, I oppose this
motion."

This speech is typical of Pitt's methods and manner. In
its manly and dignified tone, in its firmness in maintaining
his own position, yet fairness in considering the views of his
antagonists, in its logic, its appeal to practicality, and its emotional conclusion, it could be matched at practically every
point from dozens of his addresses. It shows in epitome
the persuasive Pitt. The conclusion must be that Pitt's
persuasive effectiveness was not of the highest, but that he
showed a complete mastery over his technique which was
unusual. Fox made the significant admission that in a
twenty-year's contest with Pitt he never once caught him
tripping. Pitt was the artisan who always knew what he
was about.

Part Five

Retrospect

Chapter 14 — A Summary View

An observer in the galleries of the House of Commons during any session of the years from 1781 to 1794 might have seen four of England's greatest speakers together. The time would probably have been late evening, for the business of the House did not get well under way until four o'clock in the afternoon, and the important speeches were delivered after the dinner hour. Several of the greatest efforts of modern eloquence were delivered after two in the morning, and some of the greatest speeches were finished after sunrise. Even from the gallery, the visitor would have been aware of a distinct odor of wine, for almost all of the members were fond of the bottle.

In the midst of the ministerial circle there could be observed the tall, thin, dignified, austere figure of Pitt, watching with cold calmness the strategy of the Opposition. On the benches across the hall, Burke would be seated, with Sheridan and Fox on either side of him. Or, if the debate had lasted very long, Fox would be rolling his huge bulk around the hall, talking and laughing with the other members, friends and foes alike. Sheridan, too, would probably be talking with friends, but not Burke. A contemporary, comparing Burke and Fox, remarked that "The one procured admirers, the other possessed friends."

Of the four, Burke was easily the greatest stylist, both in the magnificence of his conceptions and in the grandeur of his verbal images. Fox was admittedly the more effective debater, because of the quickness and clarity with which he discovered and exposed the weaknesses in his opponent's arguments. Although in both logic and proof 'Fox was often inferior to Burke, he had greater skill in emphasizing his main ideas. Furthermore, the impetuous sincerity of his manner helped greatly to carry his points.

Sheridan's greatest forensic weapon was his wit, which he used sometimes in rapier-like, good-humored, satirical thrusts into the weak spots of his opponent's armor, or as a heavy bludgeon of withering sarcasm to overwhelm him. Pitt was always in perfect control of himself. Even when he had drunk heavily of port wine, he was able to use his keen perception and unexampled fluency to full advantage. Whether clarifying the intricate problems of finance, or skillfully beclouding the issues so his Tory adherents could not understand them, he kept his followers in line.

Burke represented the fullness of mind of the historical scholar and political philosopher. Fox combined the versatility of the classical student and the cleverness of the convinced opportunist. Sheridan presented the careless brilliance of the hard-working artist, who was apparently more concerned with style than subject matter, yet keeping his listeners attentive to the point he sought to establish. Pitt, for all his virtues, revealed the narrow concentration of a mind that from early childhood had been directly and unfalteringly intent upon the task of gaining and maintaining control of the House of Commons.

Burke was a moderate Whig who believed in rule by the best, rather than by the majority. He favored reform, but shrank from revolution. An innate prudence restrained him from too great liberalism. His legislative career resolved around the reform of the governments of Ireland, the American colonies, and India; control of the revolution in France; the punishment of Warren Hastings; economic reforms in the English government; Catholic emancipation, abolition of the slave trade, and development of free trade. His legislative theory was neatly summarized in his statement to his Bristol constituency, when he said in effect, "Your representative owes you not his vote merely, but his judgment and his integrity."

Fox was a staunch liberal who believed strongly in freedom and majority rule. In the pursuit of reform, he was enthusiastic to the point of rashness. His legislative career was checkered and sometimes contradictory. Among the many reforms he advocated, special mention should be given to the strict limitation of royal authority, reform of the electoral system, liberalization of the governments of Ireland and India, freedom for the American colonies, support of the French Revolution, abolition of the slave trade, emancipation of Catholics, and freedom of the press. His epitaph could well be drawn from his speech of February 17, 1783, when he said, "It is not in my nature to bear malice, nor to live in ill-will. My friendships are perpetual,

my enmities are not so." He abjured in word and in prac-
ties "those behind-hand and paltry maneuvers which
destroy confidence between human beings, and degrade the
character of the statesman and the man."

Sheridan verged on radicalism. His advocacy of his
principles was often violent to the point of ineffectiveness.
The causes to which he gave thirty years of his life included
anti-militarism, freedom of the press, abolition of slavery,
home rule for Ireland, parliamentary reform, reform of
penal laws, free trade, strict limitation of the English monarchy, and outspoken support of even the excesses of the
French Revolution. Remembered now almost solely as a
dramatist, it was as a legislative speaker that he sought to
establish a lasting reputation. Although he denounced,
"severity of epithet . . . redundancy of egotism . . . and
pomp of panegyric," these were undoubtedly characteristics
of his own speaking. But he was right in insisting that he
was "the mouthpiece of no party . . . nor was he the tool of
any party." An able and successful man of literature, he
entered politics not for what he could get, but for what he
could give. His speeches deserve to be resurrected for their
brilliance and wit, if not for prudence and wisdom.

Pitt, although forced by circumstances into leadership of
the Tory party, was at heart a moderate Whig. It is not
unnatural that he and Burke were at last united. Extremely patriotic and reverent toward monarchy, Pitt's
greatest achievement was his restoration of ministerial authority. In international affairs, his aim was to maintain
English dominance through establishment of a European
balance of power. Hence he opposed Napoleon, sought
the restoration of the Bourbon dynasty in France, and labored to cement a Prussian-Dutch alliance. His chief weak-

ness was his unwillness to sacrifice popularity for his principles. Consequently, he was moderate in his advocacy of parliamentary and economic reforms, in his concessions to Catholics, and in seeking abolition of the slave trade. Following his father's lead in electoral reform, he sought the middle ground of compensating the "owners" of the rotten burroughs, and never fully trusted the principle of majority rule.

In their personalities, beliefs, and methods these four were very dissimilar. Through their interaction upon the same stage is presented an excellent opportunity to analyze various types of parliamentary effectiveness. From the examination of their careers it would appear that strength of intellect, intensity of purpose, and concentration upon the means of influencing audiences through speech are of more importance to a political leader than the external qualities of personal appearance or the accident of family or social position. Each in his way was a very great man. In their personal appeal and the extent of their influence, they have not often been surpassed.

APPENDIX A: BIOGRAPHICAL TABLE

In the following pages, the chief biographical material concerning Burke, Fox, Sheridan, and Pitt is presented in tabular form, in order that it may be possible at a glance to determine the relative positions of the four in any year. Only material significant in the growth of their personalities and characters, and to their development and progress as speakers is included:

BURKE	FOX
1730 Born, Dublin, January 1, son of a reputable protestant barrister and a Catholic mother. Being a delicate child, he spent his childhood reading, rather than in sports.	
1741 Went to school at Ballitore, kept by a Quaker master, A Shackleton, for whom Burke long retained a close attachment.	
1744 Was admitted to Trinity College, Dublin, where he remained for six years, studying hard in classical and English literature, philosophy, and political science. He proceeded A. M. in 1751.	
1749	Born, January 24, son of the corrupt politician, Henry Fox, and Lady Georgiana Lennox, descendant of Charles II. His father reared him with every indulgence, letting the boy's caprice be law. He deliberately taught him to gamble, as well as training him in statescraft and oratory.
1751 Commenced the study of law in the Middle Temple, London. However, he was not attracted by it, and the necessity of earning his living turned him to literary pursuits.	

SHERIDAN   PITT

Born, September, in Dublin, son of the
    great elocution teacher and lexi-
    cographer, Thomas Sheridan, and
    a mother who was an authoress of
    note. His father was very im-
    provident, and Sheridan's youth
    was one of alternate plenty and
    poverty.

BURKE

FOX

1756 His *Vindication of Natural Society*, written in the style of Bolingbroke, was widely accepted as a posthumous work of that nobleman.

At his own request he was sent to school to M. Pampellone, who conducted a school for boys of high rank.

His *Essay on the Sublime and Beautiful* was called by Dr. Johnson "a model of philosophic criticism," and won him a wide reputation.

1757 Married a daughter of Dr. Nugent, of Bath, and published a two-volume *Account of the European Settlements of America.*

1758

Admitted to Eton, where he was studious and popular.

1759

1761 Returned to Ireland as private secretary to Wm. G. Hamilton, who was secretary of State for that island.

1762

1763 After a quarrel with Hamilton, Burke returned to England.

His father took him to Paris and Spa, and encouraged him in prodigal gambling.

1764

Entered Hertford College, Oxford, where he studied hard in the classics and mathematics.

1765 Became the private secretary of the Marquis of Rockingham, and was returned for parliament for the borough of Wendover. He purchased his estate at Beaconsfield for aboout 20,000 pounds.

1766 In January he made his first speech in parliament, opposing the Stamp Act. He was highly praised by Lord Chatham.

Left Oxford, travelled on the continent.

SHERIDAN   PITT

Born, May 28, at Hayes, son of Lord
Chatham, and Lady Hester Grenville, Countess of Temple. He
was a very weak child, so studied
at home under a private tutor,
Rev. Edward Wilson.

Entered Harrow, where he was popular
with the students and the teachers,
but studied little.

BURKE

FOX

1768

In March his father purchased for him a seat in parliament for the borough of Midhurst.

He took his seat in November, before he reached his majority. He commenced as a warm Tory and an enemy of popular rights.

1770

Was made a lord of the admiralty in Lord North's g o v e r n m e n t. Throughout this year and the next he made himself very unpopular by attacking freedom of the press.

1771 Was appointed agent for the colony of New York, at a salary of 700 pounds; he held this office until the outbreak of the American war.

1772

Resigned office in order to oppose the Royal Marriage Bill, but in December he re-entered the administration.

1773

1774 On April 19 he electrified the House with his speech on American Taxation.

On February 24 he was curtly dismissed from office for offending the king. He had gambling debts of 140,-000 pounds which his father paid. In this year his father, mother, and elder brother died. Fox joined the Opposition.

1775 On March 22 he delivered his speech on Conciliation with the Colonies.

On February 2 he made his best speech to date, attacking the American war. He continued to speak often and warmly on this subject.

SHERIDAN   PITT

Eloped to France with Miss Linley, a celebrated beauty of Bath. They were remarried the following year.

At the age of fourteen he entered Pembroke College, Cambridge, where Geo. Pretyman became his tutor. Pretyman was to serve Pitt as private secretary during most of his later life, and wrote his biography. Pitt studied very hard in the classics, and mathematics. His health continuing poor, he was ordered to drink port wine, and developed an immoderate taste for it, which continued throughout his life. It was almost his only vice.

Commenced the study of law, but soon abandoned it. He was saved from destitution by a gift of 3,000 pounds from one of his wife's rejected suitors. He refused to permit her to support them by singing.

On January 17 he brought forth his play, "The Rivals," at Convent Garden Theatre.
He followed it with an opera, "The Duenna," both of which were very popular.

Heard his father speak in parliament for the first time. Hereafter, he often attended the parliamentary debates.

1776

1777

1778 Speech on Burgoyne's use of In-   His enemies through the *Morning Post*
     dians.   tried to force him into a duel with
                                              Colonel Lutrell, who was a deadly
                                              shot. On February 2 he spoke
                                              for almost three hours in seathing
                                              review of the ministry's war
                                              policy; a speech to which no re-
                                              ply could be, or was, made.

1779

1780 On February 11 he delivered his   Was chairman of a mass meeting de-
     speech on Economical Reform. In   manding parliamentary reform. He
     September he lost his seat for   also spoke against the influence of
     Bristol, and was returned for the   the crown, and for Catholic
     pocket borough of Malton.   emancipation.

1781 On November 27 he delivered   Was impoverished by his gambling, and
     one of his best speeches against   his library was sold for debt.
     the war.

1782 Was excluded from the Rocking-   Entered the Rockingham Cabinet as sec-
     ham cabinet, but got his reform   retary of state, and resigned in
     bill passed.   July when Shelburne became min-
                                              ister.

1783 As a member of the Coalition   Formed the ill-starred, odious coalition
     Government he spoke for the East   with North, which put him in
     India Bill on December 1.   office from April-December, when
                                              the use of "secret influence" by
                                              the king destroyed his India Bill,
                                              and dissolved the government.

SHERIDAN

Purchased Garrick's interest in Drury Lane Theatre, and became its manager.

Produced his greatest success, "The School for Scandal."

PITT

Upon the death of his father, Pitt was left with an income of only 300 pounds, and commenced the study of law.

Produced "The Critic," the last of his great dramatic productions.

Appeared with Fox at the Westminster meeting for parliamentary reform, and achieved his ambition of entering parliament. He was elected for Stafford at an election cost of 2,000 pounds. He made his maiden speech on November 20 of this year, defending himself against charges of corrupt electioneering.

Was admitted to the bar, and rode the western circuit. In the elections of this year he stood for Cambridge, but was last on the poll. He was returned for the pocket borough of Appleby.

Took his seat in January, and during the session won a high reputation as a speaker with three addresses. In November he made a strenuous attack upon the American war.

Served as Under-Secretary of State under Rockingham, and made his famous "Angry boy" retort to Pitt.

Disdainfully refused a minor position in the Rockingham government, saying he would accept nothing but a cabinet position. In July he entered the cabinet under Shelburne.

Served in the Coalition government as secretary of the treasury.

Upon defeat of Fox's India Bill, Pitt was appointed prime minister.

BURKE

FOX

1784

His followers became "Fox's Martyrs" in an election which swept 160 of them out of parliament. Fox himself was barely re-elected for Westminster, after a hard campaign. His election was disputed, and on June 3 he gave his great speech on the Westminster Scrutiny.

1785 On February 28, he delivered his speech on the Nabob of Arcot's Debts, the last of the six he wrote out for publication. Later in the year, he commenced his movement to impeach Hastings.

1786 Precipitated the impeachement of Hastings with his speech on Cheyte Sing.

1787 On April 25 the articles of impeachment were submitted by Burke to the House and accepted. His speech lasted three days, and had a tremendous effect. The trial did not end until 1794, when Hastings was acquitted.

Was made one of the managers of the Hastings impeachment.

1788 Became very intemperate in his demands for a Regency during the King's temporary insanity.

Hastened home from Italy to take part in the Regency battle. His bold advocacy of the right of the Prince of Wales to the Regency lost him many friends.

1789 Sensed danger in the very beginning of the French Revolution.

Hailed the French Revolution as the greatest and best event that had occurred in the history of the world.

1790 In February, quarrelled with Fox in parliament over the Revolution. In November he published his *Reflections on the Revolution in France*, of which 30,000 copies were sold immediately; the book did much to precipitate England into the war.

Brought forward his bill giving juries power to determine guilt as well as facts in libel trials.

SHERIDAN	PITT
	Won a large majority of the House in the elections of this year.
On May 30, he made a strong speech against the Irish Commercial bills.	Brought forward his plan for parliamentary reform, which was defeated. Also proposed eleven resolutions which would have granted free trade to Ireland at the cost of her legislative freedom. They were defeated. In his budget speech, he proposed his plan for a Sinking Fund to pay off the national debt. It was accepted, and, with his policy of increased taxes and reduced expenditures, did greatly reduce the debt. By his consent he made possible the impeachment of W. Hastings.
On February 7, he delivered his greatest speech, indicting Hastings on the Begums charge. He won unrivalled fame by it. He was appointed one of the managers of the impeachment.	In pursuance of his policy of free trade, Pitt secured a commercial treaty with France.
On June 3-13, Sheridan repeated his Begum's speech in Westminster Hall, before the Lords. Participated actively in the Regency battle.	
On February 9, Sheridan intemperately attacked Burke, thus hastening the split in the Whig party.	Settled a dispute with Spain over Nootka Sound, without going to war.

BURKE

1791 In the debate on the Quebec Bill, May 6, he again quarrelled with Fox over France, and led his following of the "Old Whigs" over to Pitt.

1792

1793

1794 Withdrew from parliament. H i s son died, causing him great grief.

1795 Was granted a pension of 3,700 pounds, which drew upon him an attack, and his noble defense, "Letter to a Noble Lord."

1796 Added fuel to the flames of war with his "Thoughts on a Regicide Peace," which were continued into 1797.

1797 Died in his sixty-eighth year, on July 9.   —

1798

1799

1800

FOX

Prevented Pitt from leading England into a war with Russia in the dispute over Ockzakow. He brought up his libel bill again.

Moved the impeachment of Pitt on March 1, for his blundering in the dispute with Russia. His libel bill was passed, and resulted in greatly increased freedom of the press.

Commenced an opposition to the war with France which continued throughout his life. He attacked the measures of suppression which Pitt introduced during the next seven years. His friends purchased an annuity for him.

On May 26 he delivered his great speech for Parliamentary Reform.

At the Whig Club he toasted to "The Sovereignty of the People of Great Britain," an ambiguous phrase that won him great unpopularity.

Returned to parliament to deliver, on Feb. 3, his condemnation of Pitt for rejection of Bonaparte's peace overtures.

SHERIDAN	PITT
	Almost declared war on Russia, being prevented only by Fox's opposition.
His wife died.	Delivered an eloquent speech on April 2 against the slave trade.
	Reluctantly, for it meant the failure of his plan to reduce the national debt, Pitt entered the war against France. The next few years are filled w i t h subversive measures which he felt were necessary to prevent a revolution in England.
On January 21, in reply to Lord Mornington, Sheridan made his greatest speech denouncing the war against France. On May 4, he spoke in rebuttal on the Begum's charge. On January 5, he made his best speech against the suspension of the Habeas Corpus Act. Married Miss Ogle.	
	His efforts to make peace with France failed.
When the Mutiny of the Nore threatened disruption of the English navy, he rose above partisanship to give Pitt his full support.	One of England's blackest years. Pitt was forced to suspend specie payments. He again futilely sought peace. On November 10 he gave one of his best speeches on this failure of negotiation.
Wrote "Pizarro." On February 10 he made a severe attack on Pitt's war policy.	On February 3 he conducted his famous debate with Fox on his refusal to accept Napoleon's peace overtures.

BURKE   FOX
1801

1802

1803   Made one of his great speeches against
                                     the declaration of war on May 18.

1804

1806   On February 5 he again became secre-
                                     tary of state for foreign affairs.
                                     His great achievement was in pass-
                                     ing a bill to abolish the slave
                                     trade, an evil against which he
                                     had struggled valiantly for twenty
                                     years.
                                     Died on September 13, in his fif-
                                     ty-seventh year.

1809

1812

1816

SHERIDAN

PITT

In February, he resigned, because the
king would not let him keep his
promise of granting emancipation
to the Irish Catholics.

On December 8, at the expense of all
consistency, he threw his support
to the war party. He helped to
oust Addington with quip about
"doctor Fell."

On May 12 he was again made prime
minister.

Entered the government in the Grenville
Ministry, as treasurer of the navy.

Died on January 21, in his forty-seventh
year. He was buried in Westminster
Abbey and parliament voted 40,-
000 pounds to pay his debts.

Was utterly ruined financially by the
burning of Drury Lane Theatre
on February 24.

Made his last speech in parliament, and
was defeated in the general elections.

Died on July 7, at the age of sixty-
four, and was buried with great
pomp in Westminster Abbey, in
marked contrast to the heavy
cloud under which he had spent
his last years.

APPENDIX B: BIBLIOGRAPHICAL NOTE

The materials needed for a study of these men and their times may be classified in four categories. The first includes copies of their speeches, letters, writings, and other personal revelations. The next contains the diaries, journals, letters, and books of reminiscence by their contemporaries who knew them personally and heard them speak. A third source must be the biographies and histories of the time written by writers who lived through the period and thus knew it intimately. The fourth category consists of historical and biographical writings from later periods, when the judgment of the critics had been tempered and given perspective.

The first class of materials is for these four speakers particularly unsatisfactory. The texts of their speeches are only approximations of what they actually said on the floor of Parliament. Burke considerably revised those speeches that he published. None of the others ever prepared more than one or two speeches for the press, and the texts of their speeches are merely the approximations taken down by reporters who did not try, or were unable, to take verbatim notes. Both Burke and Fox left letters of real value in revealing their personalities, and Burke's political writings are very helpful in aiding the understanding of his views and development. One could wish, however, for much more of personal revelation from all four of them.

The second class of material is as rewarding as the first is disappointing. It was an age of self-conscious diarists. A great many discerning men and women prided themselves upon observing and recording the personalities and incidents that would best mirror their age. Their diaries, letters, and reminiscences parallel roughly the newspaper commentators who write daily columns of personal observation today, with the significant difference that the eighteenth century observers had not been trained in a journalistic tradition of sensationalism. From Miss Berry, Hannah More, and Fanny Burney, from Horace Walpole, Carl Philipp Moritz, and Samuel Rogers, from Sir Nathaniel William Wraxall, James Boswell, and Lord Holland, from Lady Sarah Lennox, Lady Elizabeth Lennox, and Harriet Martineau, from Junius, Coleridge, and De Quincey – and from many more besides – we have glimpses as intimate as any we might have had had we lived in London political society of that age ourselves. Their records are rich substance from which to draw.

Of critical and personal writings by participants or immediate successors to the time there are also many examples. Prior's *Burke*, Trotter's *Fox*, and the historical sketches of Lord Brougham are justly well known. The writings of Byron, Cunningham, Lord Mahon, Lord John Russell, Sir Walter Scott, Earl Stanhope, and many others are also helpful.

In the fourth category are all the many studies made by latter-day historians. Many are good, but it is no derogation of the others to cite as indispensibly helpful the works by Lecky, Traill, Sir Leslie Stephen, the two Trevelyans, and J. Holland Rose.

BIBLIOGRAPHY*

Adolphus, John. *History of England from the Accession of George the Third to the Conclusion of Peace* 1760-83. London; Cadell and Davies, 1805.

Andrews, J. *Memoirs of the Life and Reign of George the Third.* 2 vols. London; T. Kinnersley, 1820.

Anonymous. *Beauties of the Brinsleiad.* London; John Stockdale, 1785.

British Public Characters of 1798. London; R. Phillips, 1798.

Public Characters of 1799-1800. London; R. Phillips, 1807.

Defence of the Rockingham Party and Their Late Coalition with the Rt. Hon. Frederic Lord North. London; J. Stockdale, 1783.

Dialogue on the Actual State of Parliament. London; J. Stockdale, 1783.

Fox's Martyrs, or a New Book of the Sufferings of the Faithful. London; J. Whitaker, 1784.

History of the Trial of Warren Hastings, Esq. . . Containing the Whole of the Proceedings and Debates in

*Works cited only incidentally are not included in this bibliography.

184

Both Houses of Parliament . . . from February 7, 1786, *until His Acquittal, April* 23, 1795. London; 1796.

Letter to the Rt. Hon. William Pitt upon the Nature of Parliamentary Representation. London; J. Stockdale, 1784.

Parliamentary History of England from the Earliest Period to the Year 1803. Volumes 16-36 include the years 1765-1803. London; T. C. Hansard, 1813.

Armagh, William. "Edmund Burke." *Living Age,* 249 (April 7, 1906): 48-56.

Babbitt, Irving: "Burke and the Moral Imagination." *Democracy and Leadership,* pp. 97-116. Boston; Houghton Mifflin, 1924.

Baumann, Arthur A. *Burke: The Founder of Conservatism, a Study.* London; Eyre and Pottiswood, 1929.

Bernbaum, Ernest. *English Poets of the Eighteenth Century.* New York; Scribner's, 1918.

Berry, Mary. *Extracts from the Journal and Correspondence of Miss Berry* (1783-1852). Edited by Lady Theresa Lewis. 3 vols. London; Longmans, Green, 1865.

Boas, Ralph Philip, and Hahn, Barbara M. *Social Backgrounds of English Literature.* Boston; Little, Brown, and Co., 1926.

Borchers, Gladys. *A Study of Oral Style.* Ph. D. Thesis, unpublished, University of Wisconsin. 1927.

Boswell, James. *The Commonplace Book of James Boswell.* Edited by the Reverena Charles Rogers. London; Grampion Club, 1874.

The Life of Samuel Johnson. 2 vols. in one. London; Oxford University Press, 1927.

Bowers, Claude G. *The Irish Orators*. Indianapolis; Bobbs-Merrill, 1916.

Boynton, Percy H. *London in English Literature*. Chicago; University of Chicago Press, 1913.

Brigance, W. N. "What is a Successful Speech?" *Quarterly Journal of Speech*, XI (November, 1925): 372-77.

Brougham, Henry Lord. *Historical Sketches of Statesmen Who Flourished in the Time of George III*. First Series. 2 vols. London; Charles Knight and Co., 1839.

Bryant, Donald C. "Edmund Burke on Oratory." *Quarterly Journal of Speech*, XIX (February, 1933): 1-18.

"Edmund Burke's Opinions of Some Orators of His Day." *Quarterly Journal of Speech*, XX (April, 1934): 241-254.

Burke, Edmund. *Correspondence of the Right Honourable Edmund Burke; Between the Year 1744, and the Period of His Decease, in 1797*. Edited by Charles William, Earl Fitzwilliam, and Sir Richard Bourke. 4 vols. London; F. and J. Rivington, 1844.

Works. Edited by Judge Willis, with a Preface by F. W. Raffety. 6 vols. London; Oxford University Press (Oxford World Classics Series), 1925.

Buchanan, Paul S. "Logic or Bunkum in Persuasion." *Quarterly Journal of Speech*, XI (April, 1925): 157-162.

Byron, George Gordon, Lord. *Letters and Journals*. Edited by Rowland E. Prothero. 6 vols. London; John Murray, 1896-1901.

Chapman, N. *Select Speeches*. 4 vols. Philadelphia; Hopkins and Earle, 1808.

Chatterton, E. Keble. *England's Greatest Statesman, William Pitt*. Indianapolis; Bobbs-Merrill, 1930.

Chesterfield, Lord. *Letters to His Son.* Edited by Charles Strachey, with notes by Annette Calthorp. 2 vols. New York; Putnam's, 1925.

Cobbett. *Parliamentary Debates.* Volumes 1-7. London; Cox and Boylis, 1804-1806.

Coleridge, Samuel Taylor. *Essays on His Own Times.* Edited by His Daughter. 2 vols. London; William Pickering, 1850.

Courtney, W. P. "Isaac Barre." *Dictionary of National Biography,* III: 275a-276b. London; Smith, Elder, and Co., 1889.

Cowper, William. *Selected Letters.* Edited by the Reverend W. Benham. London; Macmillan, 1884.

Croker, John Wilson. *Correspondence and Diaries.* Edited by Louis J. Jennings. 3 vols. London; John Murray, 1885.

Cunningham, G. G. *Lives of Eminent and Illustrious Englishmen.* 8 vols. Glasgow; A. Fullerton and Co., 1839.

De Castro, J. Paul. *The Gordon Riots.* London; Oxford University Press, 1926.

De Quincey, Thomas. "Rhetoric." *Collected Writings.* Edited by David Masson. Volume X: 81-133. London; A. and C. Black, 1897.

Deschanel, Paul. "Pitt et Fox." *Orateurs et Hommes d'Etat.* Paris; Ancienne Maison Michel Levy, 1889.

Drinkwater, John. *Charles James Fox.* New York; Cosmopolitan Book Corp., 1929.

Ewbank, Henry Lee. "Approaches to the Study of Speech Style." *Quarterly Journal of Speech,* XVII (November, 1931): 458-465.

Objective Studies in Speech Style with Special Reference

to One Hundred English Sermons. Ph. D. Thesis, un-published, University of Wisconsin, 1931.

Fortesque, J. W. *British Statesmen of the Great War,* 1793-1814. Oxford; Clarendon Press, 1911.
Historical and Military Essays. London; Macmillan, 1928.

Fox, Charles James. *A History of the Early Part of the Reign of James the Second, with an Introductory Chapter.* London; William Miller, 1808.
Memorials and Correspondence. Edited by Lord John Russell. 4 vols. London; R. Bentley, 1853.
Speeches During the French Revolutionary War Period. With Introduction by I. C. Willis. London; J. M. Dent (Everyman's Library Series), n.d.
Speeches of the Right Honourable Charles James Fox in the House of Commons. Edited by J. Wright, with an Introductory Letter by Lord Erskine. 6 vols. London; Longman, Hurst, Rees, Orme, and Brown, 1815.

Fox, W. J. *Lectures to the Working Class.* Lecture VIII, vol. II. London; Charles Fox, 1845.

Freemantle, A. F. *England in the Nineteenth Century,* 1801-1805. London; Allen and Unwin, 1929.

Fritz, Charles A. "A Brief Review of the Chief Periods in the History of Oratory." *Quarterly Journal of Speech, VII* (February, 1922): 26-48.
"From Sheridan to Rush: the Beginnings of English Elocution." *Quarterly Journal of Speech, XVI* (February, 1930): 75-88.

George III. *Correspondence with Lord North, from* 1768 to 1783. Edited by W. Bodham Donne. 2 vols. London; John Murray, 1867.

Gibbon, Edward. *Autobiography.* Edited by Lord Sheffield, with introduction by J. B. Bury. London; Oxford University Press (Oxford World Classics Series), 1923.

Gilfillan, George. "Edmund Burke." *The Eclectic Magazine,* XXX (October, 1853): 201-213.

"Henry Lord Brougham as an Orator." *Eclectic Magazine,* XXXII (May, 1854): 21 ff.

"Richard Brinsley Sheridan." *The Eclectic Magazine,* XXXI (January, 1854): 19-28.

Goodrich, Chauncey A. *Select British Eloquence.* New York; Harpers, 1856.

Grafton, Augustus Henry, Third Duke of. *Autobiography and Political Correspondence.* Edited by Sir William R. Anson. London; John Murray, 1898.

Green, J. R. *A Short History of the English People.* New York; Harpers, 1895.

Greenwood, Alice D. *Horace Walpole's World.* London; George Bell and Sons, 1913.

Grierson, Herbert J. C. "Edmund Burke." *Cambridge History of English Literature,* Vol. XI, Chapter 1. New York; Macmillan, 1933.

Hannah, Robert. "Burke's Audience." *Quarterly Journal of Speech,* XI (April, 1925): 145-150.
Edmund Burke the Rhetorician, M. A. Thesis, unpublished, Cornell University.

Hardwicke, Henry. *History of Oratory and Orators.* New York; 1896.

Harrison, Frederic. *Chatham.* London; Macmillan, 1925.

Harshberger, H. C. *Burke's Chief American Works.* Ph. D. Thesis, unpublished. Cornell University, 1929.

Hill, Constance. *Fanny Burney at the Court of Queen Charlotte.* London; John Lane, 1912.

Holland, Henry Richard, Lord. *Memoirs of the Whig Party During My Time.* 2 vols. London; Longman, Brown, Green, and Longmans, 1852-1854.

Holland, Lady Elizabeth. *Journals.* 2 vols. London; Longmans, Green and Co., 1903.

Hopkins, Arthur A. *The Pitt-Fox Debate on Negotiation with Bonaparte, a Critical Study in Argumentative Discourse.* M. A. Thesis, unpublished. University of Iowa, 1928.

Howard, John. *The State of the Prisons in England and Wales.* Warrington; William Eyres, 1777.

Ilchester, Earl. *Life of Henry Fox, First Lord Holland.* 2 vols. London; John Murray, 1920.

Johnston, James. *Westminster Voices.* London; Hodder and Stoughton, n. d.

Junius. *Letters.* 2 vols. London; T. Bentley, 1799.

Kettle, T. M. *Irish Orators and Oratory.* London; T. Fisher Unwin, n. d.

Landor, Walter Savage. *Charles James Fox.* Edited by Stephen Wheeler. London; John Murray, 1907.

Lasswell, H. D. *Psychopathology and Politics.* Chicago; University of Chicago Press, 1930.

Lecky, William E. H. *A History of England in the Eighteenth Century.* 8 vols. New York; Appleton, 1887.

Lennox, Lady Sarah. *Life and Letters,* 1745-1826. Edited by the Countess of Ilchester and Lord Stavordale. 2 vols. London; John Murray.

Lodge, Henry Cabot. "The Early Days of Fox." *Studies in History.* Boston; Houghton Mifflin, 1892.

Macaulay, Lord. "William Pitt." *Miscellaneous Works.* Edited by Lady Trevelyan. Vol. 4, pp. 94-160. New York; Harpers, n. d.

MacCurn, John. *The Political Philosophy of Burke.* New York; Longmans, Green and Co., 1913.

McGrew, J. F. *A Study of the Treatment of Speech Composition by English Writers from Cox to Whately.* M. A. Thesis, unpublished. University of Wisconsin, 1926.

McKean, Dayton. "Public Speaking and Public Opinion." *Quarterly Journal of Speech,* XVII (November, 1931): 510-522.

MacKenzie, Robert. *The Nineteenth Century, a History.* New York; Harpers (Franklin Square Library), 1880.

Mahon, Lord. *History of England from the Peace of Utrecht to the Peace of Versailles,* 1713-1783. 7 vols. Leipzig; Bernard Tauchnitz, 1854.

Malthus, T. R. *An Essay on the Principle of Population; or, A View of Its past and Present Effects on Human Happiness.* 2 vols. London; J. Johnson, 1806.

Martineau, Harriet. *History of the Thirty Years Peace.* 4 vols. London; G. Bell and Sons, 1877-1878.

Mason, Alfred B. *Horace Walpole's England as His Letters Picture It.* Boston; Houghton Mifflin, 1930.

Mathews, William. *Oratory and Orators.* Chicago; Griggs and Co., 1891.

Moore, Sir John. *Diary.* Edited by Major-General Sir J. F. Maurice. 2 vols. London; Edward Arnold, 1904.

Moore, Thomas. *Memoirs of the Life of the Right Honourable Richard Brinsley Sheridan.* 2 vols. New York; Redfield, 1858.

Moritz, Carl P. *Travels in England in* 1782. London; Oxford University Press, 1924.

Morley, John. *Burke.* New York; Harpers (English Men of Letters Series), 1879.

Edmund Burke, a Historical Study. New York; Macmillan, 1867.

Mortensen, Elmer B. *The Oratorical Qualities of Richard Brinsley Sheridan.* M. A. Thesis. unpublished. University of Iowa, 1933.

Mowat, R. B. *England in the Eighteenth Century.* London; Harrap and Co., 1932.

Murray, Elwood. "An Histriometric Study of the Early Traits of Great Orators." *Quarterly Journal of Speech,* XIV (November, 1928): 502-508.

Murray, John Middleton. *The Problem of Style.* London; Oxford University Press, 1921.

Murray, Robert. *Edmund Burke, a Biography.* London; Oxford University Press, 1931.

Newman, Bertram. *Edmund Burke.* London; Bell and Sons, 1927.

Nicholl, Henry J. *Great Orators.* Edinburgh; McNiven and Wallace, 1880.

Oliphant, Mrs. *Sheridan.* New York; Harpers (English Men of Letters Series), 1902.

Palmer, Upton Sinclair. *An Analysis of the Argumentative Method of Certain Representative Speeches of Charles James Fox.* M. A. Thesis, unpublished. University of Iowa, 1930.

Parrish, W. M. "The Style of Extemporaneous Speech." *Quarterly Journal of Speech,* IX. (November, 1923): 345-358.

Phillips, Myron Gustavus. *Factors in the Training and Education of William Pitt the Younger Accounting for His Ability as a Parliamentary Speaker.* M. A. Thesis, unpublished. University of Iowa, 1931.

Pitt, William. *Orations on the French War, to the Peace of Amiens.* London; J. M. Dent (Everyman's Library Series), 1912.
Speeches of the Right Honourable William Pitt in the House of Commons. Edited by W. S. Hathaway. London; Longman, Hurst, Rees, and Orme, 1806.

Platz, Mabel. *History of Public Speaking.* New York; Noble and Noble, 1935.

Previte-Orton, C. W. "Political Writers and Speakers." *Cambridge History of English Literature,* vol. XI, Chapter II. New York; Macmillan, 1933.

Prior, James. *Life of the Right Honourable Edmund Burke.* London; Bell and Daldy, 1872.

Rae, John. *Life of Adam Smith.* New York; Macmillan, 1895.

Rae, W. F. *Sheridan.* 2 vols. London; R. Bentley, 1896. *Wilkes, Sheridan, Fox.* New York; Appleton, 1882.

Reid, Loren Dudley. *Charles James Fox, a Study in the Effectiveness of an Eighteenth Century Parliamentary Speaker.* Iowa City. Privately printed, 1932.
Factors in the Training and Education of Charles James Fox Accounting for His Ability as a Parliamentary Speaker. M. A. Thesis. University of Iowa, 1930.

Riker, Thad W. *Henry Fox, First Lord of Holland, a Study of the Career of an Eighteenth Century Politician.* 2 vols. Oxford; Clarendon Press, 1911.

Robertson, Charles G. *England Under the Hanoverians.* New York; Putnam's, 1930.

Rogers, Samuel. *Recollections.* London; Longman, Green, Longman and Roberts, 1859.

Rose, J. Holland. *Pitt and Napoleon.* London; Bell and Sons, 1912.

William Pitt and the Great War. London; Bell and Sons, 1911.

William Pitt and National Revival. London; Bell and Sons, 1911.

Rosebery, Archibald Phillip Primrose, Lord. *Pitt.* London; Macmillan, 1891.

Ruffin, J. N. *Forms of Oratorical Expression and Their Delivery.* London; Simpkin, Marshall, Hamilton, Kent and Co., 1920.

Russell, Lord John. *The Life and Times of Charles James Fox.* 3 vols. London; R. Bentley, 1859.

Sadler, Michael T. H. *The Political Career of Richard Brinsley Sheridan* (The Stanhope Essay for 1912). Oxford; B. N. Blackwell, 1912.

Samuels, Arthur P. I. *The Early Life, Correspondence and Writings of the Right Honourable Edmund Burke.* Cambridge; University Press, 1923.

Sanders, Lloyd C. *Life of Richard Brinsley Sheridan.* London; Walter Scott (Great Writers Series), n. d.

Sanford, William P. *English Theories of Public Address,* 1530-1828. Columbus, Ohio; H. L. Hedrick, 1931.

Scott, Sir Walter. *Journal.* New York; Harpers, 1891.

Scott-Waring, John. *A Letter to the People of Great Britain.* London; J. Stockdale, 1789.

Charge Against the Right Honourable Edmund Burke. London; J. Stockdale, 1789.

Seeley, L. B. *Horace Walpole and His World, Select Passages from His Letters.* New York; Scribner's, 3rd edition, n. d.

Sheridan, Richard Brinsley. *Plays and Poems.* Edited by R. Crompton Rhodes. 3 vols. Oxford; Basil Blackwell, 1928.

Speeches (Several Corrected by Himself). Edited by a Constitutional Friend. 5 vols. London; Patrick Martin, 1816.

Sichel, Walter. *Sheridan.* 2 vols. Boston; Houghton Mifflin, 1909.

Stanhope, Earl. *The Life of the Right Honourable William Pitt.* 4 vols. London; John Murray, 1861-1862.

Stephen, Sir Leslie. *History of Eighteenth Century Thought.* 2 vols. New York; Putnam's, 1927.

"Sir Philip Francis." *Dictionary of National Biography,* Vol. 20, pp. 171-ff. London; Smith, Elder and Co., 1889.

Taine, H. A. *History of English Literature,* translated by H. Van Laun. 2 vols. New York; Holt, 1874.

Tomline, George. *Memoirs of the Life of the Right Honourable William Pitt.* 2 vols. London; John Murray, 1821.

Trevelyan, George Macaulay. *British History in the Nineteenth Century,* 1782-1901. London; Longmans, Green, 1924.

Trevelyan, George Otto. *George the Third and Charles Fox.* 2 vols. London; 1912-1914.
The American Revolution. 3 vols. in 4. New York; Longmans, Green, 1899-1907.
The Early History of Charles James Fox. New York; 1880.

Traill, Henry Duff, ed. *Social England; a Record of the Progress of the People.* 6 vols. London; Cassell and Co., 1893-1897.

Turberville, A. S. ed. *Johnson's England; an Account of the Life and Manners of His Age.* 2 vols. Oxford; Clarendon Press, 1933.

Walpole, Horace. *Journal of the Reign of George III,* edited by Dr. Doran. 3 vols. London; R. Bentley, 1859. *The Last Journals.* Edited by A. Francis Steaurt. 2 vols. London; John Lane, 1910.

Wecter, Dixon. *Edmund Burke and His Kinsmen, a Study of the Statesman's Financial Integrity and Private Relationships.* Boulder; University of Colorado Studies. Series B. Vol. I, No. 1, 1939.

Welty, M. *The Place of Oratory in the Field of Fine Arts.* M. A. Thesis, unpublished. University of Wisconsin, 1926.

Wichelns, Herbert A. "The Literary Criticism of Oratory." *Studies in Rhetoric in Honor of James Albert Winans.* New York; Century, 1925.

Wilson, P. W. *William Pitt the Younger.* New York; Doubleday Doran, 1930.

Wingfield-Stratford, Sir Esme. *History of British Civilization.* New York; Harcourt Brace, 1930.

Winstanley, D. A. *Personal and Party Government* (1760-1766). Cambridge; University Press, 1910.

Woolbert, Charles H. "Speaking and Writing – A Study of Differences." *Quarterly Journal of Speech,* VIII (June, 1922): 271-285.

Wraxall, Sir Nathaniel William. *A Short Review of the Political State of Great Britain at the Commencement of the Year* 1787. London; J. Debrett, 1787.

Wraxall, Sir Nathaniel William. *Historical and Posthumous Memoirs.* Edited by Henry B. Wheatley. 5 vols. London; Bickers and Sons, 1884.

Wright, Thomas. *England Under the House of Hanover.* Illustrated from the Caricatures and Satires of the Day. 2 vols. London; R. Bentley, 1848.